This book is dedicated to late Dr.Dilip Roy (ex-reader BU) who moulded millions of minds

Contents

Introduction to First Edition

It gives me immense pleasure to introduce the book Envision Life penned by Tusar Kole – a unique book from an unusual author. I had known Tusar for many years but only as an engineering expert and an excellent manager. Perhaps his exposure to high-stake challenges and problems faced in his long and successful career honed his soft skills and helped him develop deep insights into the realm of human behaviour and responses.

The book is unique as it entails pragmatic solutions to path blockers like uncertainties, false beliefs, irrationality, judgmental biases which could block our day-to-day life. It makes suggestions to change the way we look at the events causing ups and downs in our lives, our inclination to use heuristic approach to resolve every life problems that eventually fails to produce everlasting solution remaining under the influence of false-beliefs, judgmental biases.

Tusar touches upon a wide range of inter-connected aspects be it the need of rationality and ethics or the classical question "whether natural events including creation of universe is deterministic or purely happened by chance". It also talks about Positivism as an emotional alignment for seeing things in optimistic way. The author gives its views on Dream, Perception, Myth and Reality that are the major drivers of behaviour in a professional's life and then suggests the use of mathematical models for optimal decision making. The book introduces the concept of optimal well being and life satisfaction covering the work spheres of our life like Biological, Emotional, Economic and Social well being.

The readers will find the ideas presented by Tusar, whatever be their background, give a fresh approach to view life and will certainly stimulate their thinking.

Viren Kaushik

Viren Kaushik
(Former Managing Director–Kribhco Sh. Fertilizers Ltd., Noida)
(Former Managing Director- Duncans Industries Ltd., N.Delhi)
(Former Director General – FAI, N.Delhi)
 KAUSHIK ESTATE,
Madangir Village,
BRT Corridor Road,
New Delhi – 110 062.

Ph: +91-11-46858574, Mob: +91-9999999757, E-mail: vpkaushik@gmail.com

WHAT MADE ME WRITE

Every one of us might have passed through complexity of situation blended with uncertainties, fallacies of pseudo logic, irrationality, false belief and mistaken perception and probably have encountered trouble in choosing righteous judgment while following the path of prudence.

And sometimes we got fascinated by observing some of the miracles happened to our life as well, some of the events remained inexplicable, a few of mystifying problems kept enigmatic and may be countless discontent could not be redressed. In fact, I also wonder why Mother Nature has experimented with her ultimate creation by posing such adversities; it is quite amazing how she has succeeded in culmination of its great creature, the next big thing after big bang and creation of life on earth. Just ponder, what a chaotic universe could have been there if no rules to stand for, as if planets collide planets, galaxies go off emitting the last rays of energy collapsing to a dooms day crunch, black hole sucks up matters around, the species devour another, human devastates the planet to make himself master of universe, letting the entire creation go in complete haywire. Thank nature, at least for this moment, it has not become so disorderly like primordial universe. Nevertheless, we became full-blown mutant on bending the rules of the universe and even laid down by our ancestors; we do whatever we think right and even whatever others hesitate to do, contradict set principles, justify our blunder and still the universe goes on expanding the horizon by leaps and bounds keeping the uniformity of matter and energy all over. Is it because we are at infinitesimally smaller in scale compared to size of universe and our wrongdoing in any scale has little impact on entire creation at large? So, what the heck in framing and following principles for humankind on earth? In what we claim ourselves as logical and rational, is it true to its sense?

Answers were not very clear to me, until few events had thrown me into the realm of rationality, optimism and optimized rationality.

Sept 1980. It was a dark starlit night. There was no one around our outhouse. My grandma was about to leave for her home, a few furlongs away from ours, after we, the two brothers had had our dinner. She left quietly saying 'lock the door from inside'. I felt sleepy; tumbling I proceeded to walk over the courtyard to perform our daily task. Those days, my grandma used to live with us for the whole day, to cook food for three times and help us maintaining daily chores. We used to sleep in our small two room home and grandma used to go her home at night, saying behind the same thing over and over again. That night was nothing unusual for me as it started with hackneyed nightfall followed by starry sky. I used to watch night sky at my leisure, searching for the Big Dipper constellation and their changing location with respect to North Star. As usual, I locked the latch, moved back through the courtyard, looked up and saw the most unusual thing in my life. To my astonishment, a fireball with green glow of light was coming down gliding smoothly and scattering the light all around. It was just 11. I could see the smooth decent of the heavenly object and at the same time I could affirm the reality by seeing the glowing courtyard. I reaffirmed that I was on my senses as my sleepiness was gone with the wind. I screamed with scare and amazement, but it suddenly went off. My grandma has already reached her home. Then I stared at sky for long, expecting another shocker from heaven, but nothing I could see, except blinking smile of bunch of stars. I could not sleep through the night, waiting for the day break to share the matter next day with everyone, But, I could not get any satisfactory explanation from anyone. 'Falling stars or meteors; may be!?!'- was the opinion of the public.

The most amazing thing was that I was only person who had seen the event. Irrespective of the fact whether it was really meteor or any other unidentified object, the reaction of the sighting was so much intriguing that it had opened up argument between the individual perception and relativistic truth within me. I perceived, it was like many things, which were beyond my limited understanding as there are as many as never-seen-before events in someone's life as his or her imagination could go wild. Or it might be an illusion dreamt by me which had the rarest of rare possibility. I believed that it was not necessary that any fact should be explained based only upon structured logic as imaginations can go beyond the wilful cognizance of our brain. Let that be anything on earth or extra-terrestrial being, it gave me pleasure with the sighting at the end. I kept that myth, for no reasons, because I wished to remain bedazzled for long.

With the progress of science, we started to believe, everything will be fixed with the help of it; but gradually it revealed that ever growing horizon of scientific logic will always run after mirage of unknown. Our imagination can still go faster than scientific knowledge or even faster than light. It never tries to find proof of non existence but believes the possibility of existence of anything beyond the territory of unknown, which is likely to hold good in certain framework. I felt it is not necessary to find every chemical reaction, even if it may be there, behind the exhilaration in triumph of a winner, but it is meaningful to evoke positive emotion towards achieving anything we pursue.

Yet I was not a firm believer of optimal rationality until the incident in midsummer circa 1981 which took me to path of rationality. I was sleeping that night quietly but got awaken after hearing some noise outside. I got up and rushed to main entrance of corridor and there I saw an intruder sitting beside the door with drooping head. I got so frightened that for few moments I could not speak anything neither I could open the door, but managed to rush back to bedroom. Then I screamed through window of the bedroom and could gather few neighbours outside. They assembled cordoning the boundary of house to catch hold the intruder and waiting outside for him to escape through main door. Then I thought I should have seen it vividly, as an intruder could hardly sit idle with drooping head. I glared to the figure with drooping head and it got me awestruck, it is still there but turned out to be a bag of rice and a black umbrella kept over it resembling a sitting human body. I got ashamed and could not reveal anything to the crowd who was waiting for a good catch; I just told them he was smarter enough to escape before cordoning by the crowd.

As I was negotiating with my false trigger, I was able to unfold the paradox what had been lying beneath for years since my early childhood. That incident when I was too young to be home alone and a thief broke open the door latch from outside to take away some valuables while I was in my sleep, was the key to the fear that had gone so deep rooted.

We might have seen sometimes, our logic failing to understand the happening of fateful events as well, leaving us in domain of despair that almost sucks everything. Time heals where nothing remains to revive getting relinquished from trauma that we passed through. Life events causing ups and downs leave us searching a formula that never-gets-failed which does not exist and we remain with the support of few false-beliefs and biases.

I felt, there is every reason to place mind over the matters and utmost need to explore optimal rationality in quest of possibilities, keeping aside the myths, unreal threats and judgmental biases. This book is an endeavour to translate all such reverberation in labyrinth of every corner of human brain which can lead to explore enormous possibilities.

Tusar K Kole

CHAPTER-1

Visualization: The basic understanding of possibilities

"Imagination is more important than knowledge. Knowledge is limited. Logic will get you from A to B. Imagination will take you everywhere"-**Albert Einstein**

"Imagination is the beginning of creation. You imagine what you desire, you will what you imagine and at last you create what you will." -**George Bernard Shaw**

"The truly creative mind in any field is no more than this: A human creature born abnormally, inhumanly sensitive. To him... a touch is a blow, a sound is a noise, a misfortune is a tragedy, a joy is an ecstasy, a friend is a lover, a lover is a god, and failure is death. Add to this cruelly delicate organism the overpowering necessity to create, create, create -- so that without the creating of music or poetry or books or buildings or something of meaning, his very breath is cut off from him. He must create, must pour out creation. By some strange, unknown, inward urgency he is not really alive unless he is creating." - **Pearl S. Buck**

A student of standard IV had asked me once "whose idea is it to transport seeds of plants to faraway places to spread their progenies? Are they keeping any bond and know the whereabouts of their departed offspring? Who has planned like this? Is it the plant itself or someone else?" I could not give him satisfactory answer until some of the mysteries got unravelled before me. I thought the question is not only pertinent to life science but also holds true in day to day survival and evolution of living things.

I was also suffering for long time with similar kind of thought 'what was the basis of creation and survival of plant and animal kingdom- is it founded upon exploring possibilities or dependent on random phenomena happening all around?' Probably, it's true to some extent as nature has designed some characteristics of its creation so that best possible outcome is achieved through exploration of several ways in case possibilities are low. On the other hand, nature's exploration tends to be limited if possibilities are quite bright. Reproduction of insects happens to be on large scale, as mortality rate of the species is high. Big animals are reproduced less in numbers as possibility of survival is greater. Plants bloom flowers, attract insects and birds to get them pollinated and in turn give them nectar. On ingestion of the fruits birds spread the seeds in distant places. A few had adopted obscure means to spread their seeds, such as Dynamite tree, which depends on air; their seeds burst into pieces in the air to spread out. Flowers have their bright and contrasting colour to attract insects, while the caterpillar which takes birth during winter turns into brown colour to camouflage matching foliage. All these are the examples of survival struggle the Mother Nature has designed for every species enabling them to find the possibilities out of many options available and every species has its own characteristic survival struggle and dependency on natural phenomena or on other species and they interact accordingly with their survival and growth need. Therefore, the nature has built within the species, instincts like anger and fear which are for putting the creation into combat against the animosity and cautioning themselves to protect from being endangered before certain unlawful motives of predators and competitors in the race of survival. It has too created positive emotions like, love, generosity, care and curiosity to grow and expand within certain period of life span allocated to every species in their generation creating the possibilities to turn adversities into opportunities.

The nature has also gifted us possibly with the most fabulous tools- the power of imagination; the basic necessity of advancement, to see beyond our visual world: the power of visualization.

And here are some of the revelations of the most baffling queries revolving around visualization and possibilities.

What nature has visualized about its creation?

We know it's very difficult to answer; nonetheless, it is evident that creation is ultimate manifestation of giving energy, passing on self-sufficiency into creature to progress and procreate, surely nature would have visualized beforehand that creation is not supposed only to attain certain end result but also to evolve through passage of time. It signifies means are as much important as the end; rather end is less important in bigger scenario, such as progressing on the path of evolution is more important than what anybody or anything is set to become. On the other hand, becoming whatever you like is resultant of means what you choose to pursue. If the means are numerous it is prudent to seek best possible optimistic way towards success. Mankind is having enormous possibilities but find difficulties knowing future outcome, as results are governed by the constraints which are mostly created by human race itself, mostly influenced by ulterior motives. The constraints hinder the path leading to success by pessimism whereas law of the nature ushers optimistic possibilities. It signifies that visualization is foremost criteria of imagination as it not only projects the bright pictures of future in the present scenario but also blocks the intruding pessimism which has greater potential to block the path of success.

Is creation a mere possibility?

It is thought the world around us is created, governed and is likely to be eventually ended too with optimism. Creation through so called big bang resulted in creation of matter, leading to transformation of the inanimate into simple micro-organism which is thought to be cooked in primordial soup and culminated into more complex species through evolution. The nature has given the entire creation the autonomy to procreate another, exploiting the possibilities. It has designed every organism to explore better options creating numerous opportunities to choose from, enabling species to survive and evolve. In the higher order species, like human, nature has given negative and positive emotions to protect in survival race as well so as to transform themselves to get better. To cut a long story short, nature has passed on us some autonomy which we call as 'free will' to act according to our needs but a few things kept at her disposal (call it as possibilities) which are likely to happen at nature's will. Nevertheless, nature accounts for possibilities in each stage from creation, growing up, sustenance and transformation of each organism with great magnanimity and precise calculated limits.

We may see that nature has enabled reproductive system of mammals to create millions of sperms with lock and key feature preventing multiple impregnation of ovum by allowing single sperm and shutting door for the next immediately after break through. It also prevents impregnation of ovum with spermatozoa of different species. It has designed hand and fingers for enormous versatility with awesome simplicity; perfected joints of bone structures with great reliability for entire life but with limited capacity. Nature has empowered brain to stretch the limit of physical power and to identify and process threat perception with the help of long term memory built from learning from the past so as to enable creatures in reacting to situation oppressing the logic, whenever felt necessary. On the other extreme, it has designed memory to fade out in the passage of time as we grow older enabling us to forget our pain and grief. Nature has given us the power and autonomy for taking up positive move far ahead of our basic needs. It has authorized genes to process and embed learned inputs in our successors, to pass it on to next generation and mutate itself for betterment, so that evolution is not hampered. So the creation and sustenance is a blend of our free will and exploring possibilities, in which former one can be exercised for optimization and the latter indicates predetermined order of the nature which must be explored for maximization.

What has visualization to do with the possibilities?

Minuscule change in state with respect to time while heading towards the end bears the flag of evolution. The end lies within the future which can never be predicted nor desired at all to be predicted so as to make the hope and optimism stand tall against the setbacks in path of progress. This optimism gives everyone the impetus to drive towards future. Nevertheless, we always try to presume future which is not really brighter or seems to be. Fear of failure has the potential of slowing down the progress or of halting before an insipid hindrance.

We may forget or undermine our enormous power of exploration of innumerable opportunities. True visualization gives us clear picture of the future which makes the path easier, comfortable and achievement gets time bound. It is to be always remembered the outcome of any event, whatever be the form, is designed by the nature to be for betterment. Even the world might collapse in a big crunch leading to absolute singularity once again and will eventually lead to another big bang for creation of fresh new universe and so on and so forth.

Now let us understand what visualization is meant for. Visualization is the simulated and perceived realization in human brain without having any real physical sensing through sensory organ or even by virtue of past experience. It does not confine to visual sense only but encompasses the senses of listening, touching, smelling and senses of tasting also. Things can be seen without eye, can be smelt without nose and can be felt without touch and so on.

You might have seen a dream about yourself sitting in an exam which was very tough and nothing could be answered by you. These dreams generally occur when the exams are ahead and you are not well prepared. You might also have dreamt of nightmare about falling off from height or suffocating within confined space and you are suddenly awaken to discover that you really had difficulties in breathing due to bad posture. These are not meant to be ideal visualization.

The visualization is far from day dreaming and nightmares. It ensembles a picture comprising of every details perfected by its composition, form, colour, outline, characters, date and time and location embossed over it. The visualization should be nothing less than this.

But, how to visualize and is there any steps to follow or it comes only through naturally and spontaneously?

Although visualization is a natural and congenital characteristic of human being, it can be enhanced and sharpened by the skills and learned experiences from the environment to the extent one can foresee the future with amazing accuracy. We are constantly being fed with zillions of inputs into our brain. Some of inputs remain as a permanent scar in the brain. If the inputs are stored as long term memory then it can influence our reactions in the event in future, similar to one which we have come across. The reactions are composed by brain with juxtaposition of several valuable ingredients from other events also. Let us explain this with the classic John Godfrey Saxe's poetry of nineteenth century.

It was six men of Indostan
To learning much inclined,

Who went to see the Elephant
(Though all of them were blind),
That each by observation
Might satisfy his mind.

The First approach'd the Elephant,
And happening to fall
Against his broad and sturdy side,
At once began to bawl:
"God bless me! but the Elephant
Is very like a wall!"

The Second, feeling of the tusk,
Cried, -"Ho! what have we here
So very round and smooth and sharp?
To me 'tis mighty clear
This wonder of an Elephant
Is very like a spear!"

The Third approached the animal,
And happening to take
The squirming trunk within his hands,
Thus boldly up and spake:
"I see," quoth he, "the Elephant
Is very like a snake!"

The Fourth reached out his eager hand,

And felt about the knee.
"What most this wondrous beast is like
Is mighty plain," quoth he,
"'Tis clear enough the Elephant
Is very like a tree!"

The Fifth, who chanced to touch the ear,
Said: "E'en the blindest man
Can tell what this resembles most;
Deny the fact who can,
This marvel of an Elephant
Is very like a fan!"

The Sixth no sooner had begun
About the beast to grope,
Then, seizing on the swinging tail
That fell within his scope,
"I see," quoth he, "the Elephant
Is very like a rope!"

And so these men of Indostan
Disputed loud and long,

Each in his own opinion

Exceeding stiff and strong,

Though each was partly in the right,

And all were in the wrong!

Suppose these six blind persons decide to describe it to a painter (a normal person who has never seen an elephant), for a picture to be drawn on the basis of their inputs. What will be the outcome?

Obviously, the painter would draw four legs, a pair of teeth and body, but he would also add one head with two eyes and one tail which he has seen in almost all animals except elephant. Although he cannot draw the perfect picture of elephant, but he would obviously draw a picture with the inputs from blind men which resembles supernatural creature with the metamorphosis of the original (like the picture as illustrated above). The act of imagination while painting the elephant by the artist is an example of his own visualization of elephant.

We know very well, it is possible to create a near perfect picture of unseen or unknown objects very close to original based on description and with the power of imagination. Skills and prior experiences matter most for achieving near perfection in constructing any unimaginable object or living thing.

How relevant is Visualization for us? Who need it?

Every art form is created out of elements available in the nature. Artist's task is to permutate a zillion notes one after another to compose a music or placing one object beside the other, combining proper colour and tone to compose a painting. The artist renders his imagination in numerous ways but much of his or her task is eased by visualization. The selection of inputs, putting them together to create an art is simply impossible without imagination.

A student tries to memorize by verbalization and visualization technique. It is now well proven that visualization is a far better memory tool than verbalization. Our brains are evolved naturally to decode complex stimuli like pictures, colours, structures, sounds, tastes, facial expression. Even child can recognize and differentiate about 200 facial expressions of his or her mother. But in present times we have to encounter sophisticated media like print which is developed by mankind for expression of thought by combination of texts, thus our brains are not fully accustomed to memorize easily the written texts to memorize, whereas we can memorize the underlying story it tells about. Therefore it calls for visualization or attaching a visual tag to associate the written text to recall it in easier way. An apple does not mean much to us as an word comprising of letters 'a', 'p','p','l' and 'e', rather than resembling a fruit or even a computer brand.

If you are professionals in the field of engineering, architecture, cinematography you have to have your skill of visualization honed to shape the idea for forging them into reality. Technical calculations and code guidelines are meant for providing minimum criteria for design to engineers but it is amazing that for aesthetics of any creation, there is no such code available; rather visualization is the only available means to shape the creation to its completeness.

A few case studies will obviously help understand how powerful visualization is.

Case Study: Basketball experiment

An Australian psychologist, Alan Richardson had conducted an experiment to show the power of visualization in developing basketball throwing skill highlighting how visualization enhances skill even without real practice.

He formed three groups of basketball players and tested for their abilities for free throw into the net.

1st group practiced every day 20 minutes

2nd group was not allowed to practice but put to visualize making free throws.

3rd group did neither practiced nor visualized.

The result was quite amazing. The group who only visualized was found as good as those who practiced.

Case study: Mental Chess

Natan Sharansky, a Soviet-born Israeli politician and a computer specialist who had been captured as a suspected US spy in Russia and spent 9 years in prison, has served as Chairman of the Executive of the Jewish Agency since June 2009. In his childhood, he was a chess prodigy and displayed simultaneous and blindfolded chess play and he used to do a lot of experiment with mental practices. While in solitary confinement in prison, he played with himself in mental chess and began to think he might as well become the world champion. Amazingly, Sharansky beat the world chess champion Garry Kasparov in a simultaneous exhibition in Israel in 1996. This was magnificent display of power of visualization.

Case Study: Mental workout

Guang Yue, a physical work-out psychologist from Cleveland Clinic Foundation in Ohio, has experimented and observed people who went to the gym for work out as well as a group supposed to see them. He observed the group who performed work out, has gained 30% muscle increase whereas people who carried out virtual workouts just by seeing people exercising has gained by almost half as much (13.5%).

The above case studies prove the benefits of true visualization and up to what extent it can be achieved. In real life visualization may take different forms which emphasize the need of it in dynamic world. So let us go into details of various forms of visualization.

Visualization in still

Have you ever watched an architect or interior decorator renovating an old house? He or she is not capable of creating anything new, only he or she rearranges the things which seem to sooth your eyes. The architect or interior decorator has a solid visual thought, gets cue from the existing spatial orientation and prepare a three dimensional picture within his frame of mind, then translate into sketches for easy understanding. He uses colour, texture, space (contours, shapes) to make a striking combination as per your choice. His thought orientation is still life and 3 dimensional.

You may add or subtract dimensions to your visual thoughts. Just think of a beautiful landscape to draw and paint and your orientation will be 2 dimensional. If you add one more dimension i.e. time, your thought processing would be on time line so as to indicate change of state of object with respect to passage of time; you may travel back and forth between past and future. Wherever you are on the time line, if time is discrete, at any point of time, the picture will be still. If the visualization is continuous on a time line for a certain period of time the still life gets converted to life in motion and the conceptualization turns to be visualization in motion.

Visualization in motion

Think about a cinematographer or screenplay writer or director of a play; his works involve making a movie over a story line conceiving scene after scene in order to make a comprehensive motion picture on compiling all shots of small video clips. Translating a story line of larger time frame into a motion picture of limited time requires visualization in motion wherein a great deal of sequential frames with active motions are to be arranged for this. Each smaller shot of motions (called scenes) are shot in one go. All such scenes are cascaded in a manner so that story goes on along with central theme telling the side stories in parallel. Time line of the story is scaled down proportionately to fit length of the movie. Concept of arrangement or actor's action in each scene are based not only on the idea of cinematographer but the perception of mass at large who will be viewing and feeling the message of story are also kept in view.

Progressive Visualization

Most of us would like to know the future at the present time. There are three viewpoints in accepting the future outcome; first, you view the future as it comes to you in the passage of time and accept whether you like it or not. Second, you try to find future in more deterministic way, projecting it as an outcome of past or present actions and prepare yourself for the same. The third way is to shape the future as per your liking at the present time and prepare yourself suitable actions in the present. Obviously the third way is the most desirable one for everybody but requires visualization beyond time horizon which is focused in future course of action and possible outcomes.

Just think of a project you are going to execute in certain time frame with numerous minute activities, which must have an end result what you are deciding to choose. A large project may have more than 2000 activities which are networked together depending upon the relationships among the activities, like one may be started after completion of another; or two or three activities can run in parallel. You may construct the scheduling of project very accurately if you visualize the starting, progress and completion of each and every activity visualized in motion. Or else, you may end up with few activities completed and cannot go ahead due to resources constraints which you have not visualized beforehand.

Another possible way to visualize things of the far future, which is not tangibly felt at present, is to update the learning from the experience of near future. You may choose one option under uncertainty and proceed to the next step and realize that it was not right option; you might have the option to switch over to another. The learning from the first step may help understand the limits of the choices under uncertainty. Suppose you are to decide what crop should be sown after five years during winter season. You may choose to sow paddy, without any prior knowledge and you failed miserably. In the next turn you got an idea before cultivation, to learn about what crop is to sow when. In this way, you are able to limit choice by learning new things and apply updated knowledge in the next step. Decision under uncertainty can be better handled in this kind of visualization which is termed as progressive visualization.

Subjectivity in visualization

Visualization is influenced by person's ability to perceive and has distinct difference against others by way he puts his strong desire to work for him according to his individual stand point. Subjective visualization is thus dependent upon individualistic perception, belief, and superstition and even on intuition. The road map to any certain goal and the outcome of any activity differs from person to person and probability of occurrence of any preconceived event is largely dependent on individual perspective built up through way of looking at things and depth of observation.

Let us draw a mathematical analogy with the help of probability theorem to understand subjectivity in visualization:

Say for example, probability of occurrence of any event or achievement whatever he or she desires to become in certain time=P(A)

Probability of availability of required resources or alternatives at right time= P(R)

And Probability of making resources work at right time (or putting the resource to work exercising one's free will)= P(F)

Then, $P(A)=P(R) \times P(F)$

The above equation holds well when required resources are bountiful and he or she has free will to employ the resources. It is also true that if resources are not available at present time but can be acquired after elapse of time, t.

Therefore, if resources are not available at present time, its probability of availability of such resources turns to be subjective. The probability of making resource work (P(F)) for you at right time is also subjective, as employing free will is an entirely subjective matter. However, rendering 'free will' into a probabilistic function may contradict with conventional wisdom about free will, as it is defined as capacity of rational agents of individual to choose a course of action from various alternatives without any bias. In its true sense, free will is purely random in nature, whereas willingness to exercise free will is subjective. Therefore, this equation involves another probability (Probability of willingness to exercise free will, say P(W)) which has a binary possibility (i.e. 0 or 1). The equation becomes: P(A)=P(R)XP(F)XP(W).

Therefore, probability of achievement become zero, if P(W) is zero, even if P(R) and P(F) is very high. On the other hand if P(R) and P(F) is low, probability of achievement in certain time turns out to be less likely, even if P(W) is 1.

These probabilities become brighter whenever someone plans the objectives with respect to time, explores the opportunities to make resources and sustains on his or her goal with a drive to make resources work. Willingness depends on how someone visualizes the outcome of his or her effort. In case it is perceived that the effort will bear fruit of success and worthwhile it will drive the individual to put effort. Thus, whole lot is pivotal on the visualization in future time frame. Visualization gets affected by individual view points, values, ethical frame of mind, biases, superstition and intuition. In a nutshell, the emotional intelligence of individual plays vital role to build the mental frame work for subjective visualization. Subjective viewpoint can be made objective through rationalist thinking process, understanding and implementing the logical frame work of the problem.

Ever virtualized?

You may come across the term virtualization which is an extension of visualization that creates virtual reality to understand or create feelings of the real thing before attaining the goal. Generally it involves two or more sensory organs which make us to feel simultaneously creating a virtual understanding. "Virtual reality" has been prevailing and getting improved since invention by Judson Rosebush and other researchers in 90s, it finds application in games, entertainment and medical field. A doctor can now operate a patient from a remote place using this VR tool, which enables him to see all in display monitors and to feel realistically about force of incising with knife and stitching with needle. Some of recent 3D games with motion sensors create feedback senses to gamers like force of punch, back thrust of gun when fires virtually to game characters.

To make the understanding simpler, take note of this: If we create the drawing on the drawing board before making a component to be manufactured, it is visualization, but if we construct a working model of a machine then it is a virtualization.

We have seen the model architecture of building or housing complex before the construction, the builder is creating a visualization to make the customer feel about the project. Virtualization is extended version of visualization, although in some cases, it is impractical to create but it helps to analyze how the real thing will be at working condition.

Making a prototype or specimen before going into mass production will help understand how the final product will be effective. It is also required to develop all such prototypes for a complex new product or process which is very difficult to understand for its efficacy and requires up gradation with the experience from trials.

Does visualization has any role on the path of success?

Every steps leading to achievement has a complimentary relation with visualization. Behind each step you put forward there must be vision and objectives which interplay with your mind to control your action. We may analyze algorithm of success leading from setting the dreams to achievements which is a defined process consisting of steps weaved in a fabric of visualization. The success mechanism or the algorithm of success although differs in interpretation, the essence of it underlines how perfect should be the visualization.

Lets us discuss the case study of Apollo Moon Mission which was considered a citadel of human endeavour achieved through progressive visualization[Data Source for surface times and sample amounts: Apollo by the Numbers: A Statistical Reference (Orloff 2004)]

In 50's ever since the Soviet Union launched Sputnik-1 as the first artificial satellite to orbit the Earth, space race between USSR and USA came into existence between two nations. There was significant progress in space and moon mission starting from 60s, after that. Both the nations went into various space ventures trying to beat each other.

Although USA has initially progressed very slowly compared to USSR, however, eventually they had accomplished the moon landing mission through meticulously planned and time focused attempts through which all failures has contributed to successful safe landing of human to moon. The following are the steps which followed by them to accomplished the mission:

Mission	Launched Date	Mission goal	Mission result
Pioneer0,1, 2,3	1958	Lunar orbit	All failed re-entry
Pioneer4	1959	Lunar flyby, photo shoot	Partial success– reached escape velocity, Flyby too far
Pioneer P1,P3,P30, P31	1959 to1960	Lunar orbit	All Failed– pad explosion; destroyed
Ranger1, 2,3	1961-62	Prototype test	All Failed– reentered into earth
Ranger4	1962	Unmanned moon landing	Partial success: reached moon, crash impact – no photos
Ranger5,6	1962,1964	Moon Landing	All failed- spacecraft power/crash impact;
Ranger 7,8,9	1964-65	Lunar impact	All succeeded-captured photos

Mission	Launched	Mission goal	Mission result
Surveyor 1	May-66	Moon landing	Success– 11,000 pictures returned, first American Moon landing
Surveyor 2	Sep-66	Moon landing	Failure– midcourse engine malfunction, placing vehicle in unrecoverable tumble; crashed southeast of Copernicus Crater
Surveyor 3	Apr-67	Moon landing	Success– 6,000 pictures returned; trench dug to 17.5cm depth after 18 hr of robot arm use
Surveyor 4	Jul-67	Moon landing	Failure– radio contact lost 2.5 minutes before touchdown; perfect automated Moon landing possible but actual outcome unknown
Surveyor 5	Sep-67	Moon landing	Success– 19,000 photos returned, first use of alpha scatter soil composition monitor
Surveyor 6	Nov-67	Moon landing	Success– 30,000 photos returned, robot arm & alpha scatter science, engine restart, second landing 2.5 m away from first
Surveyor 7	Jan-68	Moon landing	Success– 21,000 photos returned; robot arm & alpha scatter science; laser beams from Earth detected

Mission	Launched	Mission goal	Mission result
Lunar Orbiter 1	10-Aug-66	Lunar orbiter	Success– 1,160km X 189km x 12 deg orbit, 208 m period, 80 day photography mission
Lunar Orbiter 2	6-Nov-66	Lunar orbiter	Success– 1,860km X 52km x 12 deg orbit, 208 m period, 339 day photography mission
Lunar Orbiter 3	5-Feb-67	Lunar orbiter	Success– 1,860km X 52km x 21 deg orbit, 208 m period, 246 day photography mission
Lunar Orbiter 4	4-May-67	Lunar orbiter	Success– 6,111km X 2,706km x 86 deg orbit, 721 m period, 180 day photography mission
Lunar Orbiter 5	1-Aug-67	Lunar orbiter	Success– 6,023km X 195km x 85 deg orbit, 510 m period, 183 day photography mission

Mission	Lunar lander	Lunar landing date	Duration on lunar surface
Apollo 11	Eagle	Jul-69	21:31
Apollo 12	Intrepid	Nov-69	1 day, 7:31
Apollo 14	Antares	Feb-71	1 day, 9:30
Apollo 15	Falcon	Jul-71	2 days, 18:55
Apollo 16	Orion	Apr-72	2 days, 23:02
Apollo 17	Challenger	Dec-72	3 days, 2:59

It is noted from the above that the mission did not yield any significant achievement until launching of Pioneer and Ranger 5 & 6. Significant achievement was achieved by Ranger 7, 8 & 9 which brought several photographs of moon impact.

If we see the mission goal and result, two important aspects are noticed.

1) Photographs were considered one of the important inputs to step further. These photographs were a means of understanding unknown territory which helped visualizing the threats and opportunities lies in that venture.

2) Progressive visualization: Goals were set progressively difficult as below:

Fly-by >>> Orbiting Crash Landing >>> Soft landing >>> Un-manned landing >>> manned landing >>> shorter stay >>> Longer stay.

Each progressive goal is separated by distinct advancement of skill or technological knowledge, namely flyby does not require velocity of vehicle, but orbiting around planet requires calculation of velocity and distance from the centre from the planet and crash landing essentially requires geometry and geographical data of planet in addition to former information.

Photographs of previous mission had helped significantly to visualize possible threats and deciding next action to take care the next mission. The Apollo moon mission has flaunted the human endeavour to concur one of the greatest challenges till date. With each failure it encountered, mission got stronger enabling the progress inch by inch ultimately towards success.

As we move through this information era, every query gets clarified within no time, leaving today's swanky things as yesterday's passé. So future is not very far from the view points of acquiring knowledge; may be just an extension of present times. Nonetheless, whatever be the progress of mankind, acquiring prior knowledge about the future will always require an eye of imagination. And the power of visualization will evolve more to reduce subjectivity built within it and probably everyone will understand importance of this tool used for exploring the possibilities.

CHAPTER-2

Imagination and Possibilities

"I believe that imagination is stronger than knowledge. That myth is more potent than history. That dreams are more powerful than facts. That hope always triumphs over experience. That laughter is the only cure for grief. And I believe that love is stronger than death."— **Robert Fulghum**

Why should anyone imagine? If someone thinks of his future, he has to look on future with reference to events happened in his past. It is true, all living things inherently feel that what happened in the past will get repeated in some point of time in future and its likelihood will go up if other environmental factors repeat the same way as it did in the past. So is the usefulness of memory which gets utilized to counteract future events.

Memory has also strong correlation with mutation which is a biological process evident in all living things, designed by the nature to get everyone to make it better equipped to combat future. Through mutation, reminiscent past turns out be a tool for fighting future animosities by the species. That is why memory comes into play for deciding actions on perplexing future events.

The nature has also imposed the aging process in such a way memory gets faded and the subject get weakened in fight for survival until it crushes to survival battle to end its lifecycle, be it against environment, disease or natural aging.

Not only everybody and everything remembers past, each smallest component of living thing gets influenced by the past events it encountered. Just think of human's immune system that consists of cells, tissues, endocrine glands and organs; these are working together to fight foreign bodies which can cause disease. Each and every living cell remembers past and imagines future. It can recognize and remember gazillions of enemies which it fought against in the past, and it produces secretions by releasing of fluids and cells to match up with to wipe out nearly all of them. Sometimes, immune system hits the wrong target unleashing a torrent of disorders, including allergic diseases, arthritis, and a form of diabetes. Since immune system sometimes assumes actions against new enemies, its action gets falsified.

Similarly, genetic predisposition in species forms a genetic characteristic influencing the possible phenotypic development of an individual organism within a species or population under the influence of environmental conditions. This predisposition is targeted towards betterment of host to suit the changing environment and it acts to remember the past events and learns new things from the present.

It is a fact that invariably the future does not repeat by itself identically and that it the essence of imagination which speaks about why it is necessary for future to be predicted or assumed in the path of progress.

Therefore, deciding about the future course of action is primarily dependent on two things: first the learning from the past and secondly modifying the strategy based on assumption derived out of likelihood of occurrence and resemblance to any past event. Imagination comes into play when assumptions are to be made on the basis of resemblance.

How do we imagine?

If we are asked to explain how we imagine, we would be baffled, because our imagination is an intuitive process which is not directly linked to cognitive process of brain. Pure imagination occurs in various parts of brain. The occipital lobe sits in the lower, back part of the brain. It contains visual cortex, which takes part to process visual information. Visualization or visual concepts may form through learned inputs from cognitive world which is blended with other sensory inputs and inputs from the past. The parietal lobe above the occipital lobe integrates sensory information, such as vision, touch and sound. It also constructs elementary building blocks from to create concepts. As it is understood, visualization must incorporate the possibilities of happening of specific events in the future which are purely a rational outcome of all events which are likely to occur, that may not be intuitive at all. Therefore our imagination about future gets entangled with our intuitive thinking process which manifested either in optimistic or in pessimistic way.

Why do we imagine optimistically or pessimistically?

In general, we rely on future to come up with favourable outcomes. In all species optimism drives it towards enjoyment of the present and creating opportunities to do more. However, everybody likes to remain in comfort zone or at least tries to create the same to stay within. Venturing outside this zone does not necessarily mean that it loves to leave that zone, but tries to create more comfort in future. But, why to create more comfort? Staying within the same level of comfort is nothing but a survival need but creating more comfort is a sustenance or growth need to combat uncertainty in future. Sometimes we fear to be a fallen angel, therefore starts creating more resources for more comfort fearing losing some of them in future.

So we do think pessimistically also. And we work hard to create more resources, to save it for future. We try to avoid indulging in comfort. The cycle gets repeated until we lose hope to live longer. So pessimism and optimism are the symptoms of life, which are getting manifested through our actions against imagined future.

We know some future events are bound to come up or repeat in us as others faced it identically. We have instincts like others, intrinsic behaviours, innate biological responses and even the cognitive responses against environmental inputs which are known to happen certainly with single outcome. Just like we know if we eat, our hunger will be addressed, if we get hurt we will feel pain, if we feel pleasure we'll smile. Some inputs have binary outcomes like, if we get scared, either we fight it or we flee from there. If we are lured by something for comfort either we go for it or forget it. Some inputs have multiple outcomes which we call it *possibilities*. We are not sure what will happen even we put same inputs. Our life have multitude of events like, raising child, investments, jobs, healthcare wherein single inputs have multiple possible outcomes, wherein crucial decision making comes into play.

So why the outcomes are multiple even if input is single?

In socio-economic scenario, an individual's response is dependent on many factors; there are majority of outcomes which cannot be defined in cause-effect relationship. Even if there is a cause behind any outcome it may be having cause-effect relationship happened out of long chain of inter-related events in the past, unconceivable by the affected individual in present time. In addition to that, a single outcome may be having multiple causes for which predictability of occurring any particular effect gets inaccurate or difficult. Say for example, a person fell down unconscious on a busy road and predictability of occurring any accident colliding head on with a particular car depends on that vehicle, and its starting time, the average speed to reach the spot, which in turn depends on the driver's decision made in the recent past to drive and at the end, the response by the driver after seeing him falling. Therefore, parameters for predictability cannot be ascertained by the particular affected person as he remained unaware of these events and the calculation of the same is complex for any individual.

Now consider, if we try to predict the fatality of that particular individual, multiple causes have potential to lead his fatality. He may be having a cardiac arrest; he may be hit by a car or may be hit by a truck coming that way. So there may be multiple causes to result in his fatality. In this case, we also understand even if predictability of fatality of a person on road by a particular cause is low, however the same by any cause on the road is high. Even if the cause of fatality is resulted out of subjectivity (driver's response of any vehicle) predictability gets raised due to large nos. of drivers one of which might be the cause of accidents.

Multiple outcomes out of single cause has also seen in our daily life where an individual can get confused with what input is to be used to get any particular result. In present days in socio-economic scenario, if we invest money in a particular form, it may turn haywire, if may turn manifold or it may remain as it is. It is because, it has something to do with other factors beyond our control, be it how the public fund getting re-invested, the macro-economy of the country and even the point of time when it is getting invested.

Therefore apparently it seems that your single input has multitude of outcomes, whereas it has various combinations of hidden inputs by others which influences the outcome.

Are the possibilities manageable?
In real life scenario, we eventually know that the future outcomes with multiple possibilities may have different likelihood for occurring to any particular event. It can be classified in three broad categories like most likely, least likely and equi-probable, based on their likelihood. It can also be classified in terms of impact on scenario like worst case, best case, pessimistically optimal, optimistically optimal etc. The outcome may also have different nature based on the relationship with input like random, causal having cause-effect relationship etc. Therefore, possibilities are dependent on how the problem is envisaged and inputs are utilized. Suppose, you have to go to Delhi from Shahjahanpur in shortest possible time. You imagine the following possibilities:

Board a Delhi bound train which normally takes six hours but schedule may get affected by rain, late running of train due to maintenance work, festival time rush and traffic congestion at Ghaziabad. You acquire the inputs with respect to aforesaid parameters like train running status, whether any festival is approaching or not, train passing status at Ghaziabad etc. Out of all inputs running status of train, train passing status at Ghaziabad are rational inputs, traffic congestion at specific time is a random event which cannot be predicted with certainty. Festival-rush although individually a non-predictable behaviour but collectively a predictable one with reference to past data.

Imagination vs rationality

Even if human race is considered the most rational animal on earth, but human rationality is far more distant if not the exact opposite of imagination. Imagination acts as pre-conceptual structure toward building up understanding of unknown or less known domain.

During the teaching- learning process, speaker projects his or her experience through metaphorical illustrations which forms connecting link between listeners' and speaker's domain of knowledge. However, when area full of uncertainty is dealt only with imagination, without any prior knowledge or experience, result will be speculative. Grossly, we may understand working out the decision making process from experience is rational process but decision making under uncertainty is imaginative process.

Therefore dealing with uncertainty certainly requires imagination or visualization of various possible outcomes and their probabilities. Rationality can be put into interplay with imagination when probability (a link between past experience and future outcome) of occurrence is introduced to resolve the uncertainty. In our day to day life, there are very few events of improbable nature which we don't need to resolve to make progress in life. Just like this; we do not have to know what will happen with the sun tomorrow, as till today it has risen; we take it for granted that the sun will definitely rise tomorrow as it did yesterday. It is prudent or rational for most of such events, to accept that the past data will repeat tomorrow or in the period far ahead. It is also a pragmatic approach to accept the principle of indifference as a tool for determining the probability whenever you do not find any clue of past occurrence. The rationality of using imagination is a blending art which requires idea of optimality and technique of posing the problem in proper manner.

CHAPTER-3

Rationality and Ethics

"The problem with today's world is that everyone believes they have the right to express their opinion AND have others listen to it.

The correct statement of individual rights is that everyone has the right to an opinion, but crucially, that opinion can be roundly ignored and even made fun of, particularly if it is demonstrably nonsense!"— **Brian Cox**

"Rationality is man's basic virtue, the source of all his other virtue."-**Any Rand Lexicon**

One of the most prominent and recent controversies over privacy vs. security (pertaining to a renowned US cell phone maker and Federal govt of USA) emerged when US govt. asked to reveal the locked content of cell phone held by a dead terrorist of San Bernardino shoot out case (2016) and the cell phone giant had taken the side of privacy. FBI requested the phone maker to build a program so as to unlock pass code for digging out the phone's content to help ongoing investigation for revealing terrorist connections and the maker is standing up against court order to protect the privacy of users.

CEO of the company wrote: "We have great respect for the professionals at the FBI, and we believe their intentions are good. Up to this point, we have done everything that is both within our power and within the law to help them. But now the U.S. government has asked us for something we simply do not have, and something we consider too dangerous to create. They have asked us to build a backdoor to the phone".

The cell phone maker has written an open letter to customers also to clarify their standpoint. Now, a series of questions comes by; is the phone maker's stand reasonable and ethical or FBI is trying to reach far beyond people's right of privacy to protect the national interest? Which is more important-security of the nation in the interest of the people at large or privacy of the cross section of people who use that particular cell phone? Whether the request of FBI and court order are following rationality?

Whatever outcome may emerge, phone maker's rationality should have taken the possible reaction of FBI into consideration, as in case request is rebuffed, FBI may go for any extent to reveal the pass code, which has more impact on user's privacy and would be out of control of phone maker.

Leaving aside the above specific case, whenever we come across the term 'rationality' it reminds us the characteristic of human being that 'man is rational animal'. It is meant by the state of being judgmental based upon pure logic, objectivity and reasonability and having adequate and universally acceptable supporting evidences behind every move is nothing but rationality. In its true sense, being really rational is a next to impossible for human kind, even though we are believed to be the most rational animal on earth. Still we, most of the times do not follow the rational path for judgment or decision making.

What is rational then? Wikipedia defines as "To be rational is generally considered to mean employing logical consistency and deriving appropriate conclusions from acceptable assumptions. Naturally, "consistency" and "appropriate" and "acceptable" all vary widely from person to person, which is one of the major problems with claiming to be "rational". Everyone will think they're being rational because they are happy with their assumptions and their own consistency."

There is a famous story of INTEL CEO Andy Grove, which would better explain the concept of rationality.

Intel's original business was manufacturing memory chips which had been proven to be non-profitable in 90s. Andy Grove and his colleague Gordon Moore discussed the matter at length. At one point, Andy suggested, "If we get kicked out and the board brings in a new CEO, what you think he would do?"

Gordon replied without hesitation. "He would get us out of the memory business."

"Okay," said Andy. "Then why shouldn't you and I walk out the door, come back, and do it ourselves?"

Since then, Andy and Gordon move INTEL out of memory chip manufacturing business to develop microprocessors and the rest is history,

People of high IQ like Andy and Gordon even caught up with irrationality or cognitive bias better termed as the "commitment effect".

In INTEL case, Andy and Gordon tried to keep an irrational commitment to keep their past identity as a memory chip manufacturer. When they changed their approach to "looking at a problem as if you are an outside party" they overcame this irrationality.

This story signifies that every human being is prone to get biased or get used to mental habits which thrown them out of reasonability; consciously or subconsciously he or she indulges in this mental lethargy which is nothing but irrationality.

Rationality vs. Ethics

We must understand that rationality forms an integral part in our value system and in ethics as well. No matter what the situation is prevailing, no matter what we desire or believe, our judgment should be rational to justify our virtue of independence, integrity, honesty and justice. In practice, we are guided by many factors, some of which are beyond of our control thereby causing deviation from ruthless rationality; but there are many ways to improve ourselves and our ethical and value system by imposing optimal rationality.

A paper delivered by noted cognitive scientist, Any Rand Lexicon, in Wisconsin Symposium on "Ethics in Our Time" in Madison, Wisconsin, on February 9, 1961 emphasizes rationality on value and ethics. He described:

• "The virtue of Rationality means the recognition and acceptance of reason as one's only source of knowledge, one's only judge of values and one's only guide to action" It means it's one's full commitment to his consciousness to accept rationality as only guiding force to decide and act upon.

• "It means a commitment to the principle that all of one's convictions, values, goals, desires and actions must be based on, derived from, chosen and validated by a process of thought—as precise and scrupulous a process of thought, directed by as ruthlessly strict an application of logic, as one's fullest capacity permits" It emphasizes that one's motive, thought process and actions are completely based upon ruthless logic to his own capacity. Individual's capacity depends on many factors, like mental framework, uncontrollable restraints like de-motivating obstacles, negative energy, psychological and emotional mind set

Cognitive Rationality

You might have understood that meaning of rationality is getting changed with the context. However, majority of us believes "rationality" is associated with the following characteristics:

1. Judgmental or reasonable.

2. Devoid of emotions,

3. No value on intuition, trust

4. Attributes are always measurable and quantifiable.

5. No value on qualitative aspect

It is obvious that in mathematics the term rationality can be wrapped in the covering of above characteristics, however, in cognitive rationality it has greater aspects than mentioned above.

Cognitive Rationality = Logical understanding of decision making by creating options through probabilistic approach

In realm of cognitive science, rationality is what close you look like a perfect reasoner. Since human race is far from being close to perfect reasoner, the measure "how close" helps to understand what improvement can be done to move closer.

Let us illustrate what characteristic a perfect reasoner has.

1. A perfect reasoner only believes in one principle at single point of time; he won't follow two contradictory things at the same time and same context. If time varies, context may get changed. His belief or assumption at any point of time is based upon logic and evidences available. He may change to another principle in different point of time which would be substantiated by clear reasoning.

2. His decision or choice does not get affected by any bias, personalized beliefs or desires. However, human being are having bounded rationality, whenever someone is influenced by individual desire or belief, he would choose accordingly avoiding a rational path. Suppose, it is proven that overeating is very unhealthy habit and which causes various lifestyle diseases, we cannot eliminate our desire with that known logic and we are prone to deviate from rational path to satisfy our desire. A reasoner would opt to eat low calorie high roughage containing food satisfying his desire and avoiding the ill effects of overeating.

3. He does have contradictions in its degrees of belief, in how confident it is about various things. It means his belief under uncertainty would follow quantifiable terms "degree of belief" based on probability theory. For example, common people very often build belief about supernatural existence over other people's superstition, myth and popular stories of urban legend but a perfect reasoner would build his belief upon concrete evidences only.

Optimal Rationality

There is an inadequacy in human brain to keep rationality in all circumstances as a foremost decision criterion because the brain is designed to process decision making not only on cognitive process, but also on emotional attributes of self and others. Pure rationality is an object of imagination but it can obviously be optimized between reasoning process and expectations. Therefore applied rationality is to evolve our brain to optimally-designed reasoning machines which considers other aspects like expectations, mathematically termed as probability along with emotional inputs to decision making.   There are many practical approaches to apply applied rationality. The following cases are to show how rationality is being affected by mental habits or biases and to clarify decision making in day to day scenario.

Reacting to threats irrationally

Whenever we are subjected to threats to our existence, character images, expectation and even uncertainties, we do react in individual way to protect our current state of being.

Consider the two cases of accidental deaths resulted out of gun shooting to known persons who tried to prank which was perceived as threat from intruders leading to unfortunate incidents.

Case:1 *Matilda Cabtree accidental death (source New York times Nov10, 1994*

Matilda Cabtree decided to play a prank on her father; as she was hiding in a closet and suddenly came out jumping to surprise him, shouting with "boo!". Mr. Crabtree picked up a .357-caliber pistol he kept loaded, and went into his daughter's bedroom. The door of the darkened closet opened, he shot her in the neck at very close range. She died about 12 hours later.

Case: 2 *Premila Lal accidental death (source Times of India Sept 9, 2013)*

In a freak accident, an 18-year-old Indian-origin girl was killed in Denver(USA), when she jumped out of a closet to surprise a friend, who shot her thinking she was an intruder. Premila Lal jumped out of a closet as a harmless joke to surprise Nerrek Galley, a 21-year-old family friend. But the noise startled the friend, who grabbed a gun and shot her. According to her father Praveen Lal "The closet opened and I think she jumped and screamed and he thought it was an intruder inside the closet, so he pulled the trigger,"

Both the cases presented above, are about a mistaken perception of threats and triggering panic button by emotional brain to override the logic acting to protect self and family members. Even, during the shooting they could not recognize who is being shot and whether it could just be a matter of surprising prank or anything else. Neither their logical brain let them get opportunity to think over rationally nor did their perception of event lead them to optimistic thought.

One more aspect for reacting to emergency, reveals in the above events is social evolution of mindset that goes for offense (using firearms) first. Easily accessible guns alleviate the barrier to utilize offensive action instead of resorting to self defence of other non-violent and rational means like calling police or neighbours, hiding to get more situational inputs, collecting circumstantial evidences to analyze or to resort to any other emotional reactions like fleeing. Local laws, social upbringing might have added fire to frying pan; and who can deny "react with offense" is the easiest short term action.

Now, consider another case of fight and flight situation where rationality was applied optimally.

Case3 *The case of a stolen car (name of characters changed)*

In 2006, one Maruti 800 car was stolen by a gang of truck robbers. The owner of the car, Singh, happened to be travelling with his colleague Kumar in his car in a foggy winter night just two days after that incident. It was around 11.30 at night, the stolen car was spotted by the owner accidentally, who was sitting by Kumar's side while travelling back home on a state high way. Singh instructed Kumar to stop his car to see closely what was happening to the halted stolen car from a safe distance. Silhouette of three persons were spotted who were seen doing some repair work at bonnet, but they fled immediately when Singh tried to apprehend. He, while getting close to stolen car felt a life threat upon him when a person slowly came out rolling down with folded hand from rear door resembling holding a handgun.

He quickly sheltered himself in a nearby factory shed. At that moment, Kumar remained alone inside his car and he managed to inform police and his fellow colleagues requesting armed security personnel from nearby factory premises.

Armed security arrived within 5 min while Kumar was waiting with preparedness to flee from the situation by keeping his car started. Singh was informed on cell phone after the situation got under control. Later on, after police came, it was revealed that three absconders who fled from spot were the gang of truck looters and assailants. The persons who spotted later on came out with folded hand was actually a victim who survived assailants' attack and was reacting with folded hand knowing that miscreants already fled from site. Astonishingly they discovered dead bodies on rear seat of other two victims who were found killed by the assailants.

The situation revealed three 'flight or flee' situation, one 'keep watch' situation and one rational decision turned all ill effects to be a good end.

The miscreants fled as soon as Singh tried to apprehend, perceiving threat for revealing the crime and being caught.

Singh, initially opted to go with 'fight' option when he did not feel any threat. When he felt the threat he chose to flee and save himself. Even if his threat perception was incorrect, he opted rightly to flee and hide.

The third alive victim, when he realized the assailants had fled from the spot, he gets himself out from the stolen car, and however, when he perceived a possible encounter with the unknown persons, he folded his hands for saving his life and fled to hide nearby.

Kumar opted to rational decision 'Alert' mode as he perceived being just outside the threat horizon, not getting himself outside his car. He was also well prepared to flee but when he saw gunned security men came at right time, he switched over to 'normal' mode.

The day after was full of more interesting events. The police were investigating the evidence and arranging the clue to resolve murder mystery. Since the stolen car was surprisingly spotted out by owner himself, suspicion was mounted on him. However the only alive victim acted rationally as he came out from hiding and disclosed every fact before police.

Reacting over events or objects bearing resemblance

In recent times, you might have heard of a god man whom you earlier believed to be a noble man, and recently he is found guilty with sexual abuse against a minor. Suppose, you come across another, who has not really committed a crime. But you may tend to see the second god man with same character, at least you suspect his movement and you may become profound believer that every god man has similar criminal mindset which is hidden behind his public face. Your belief is likely to get profound when you find another (third) god man with similar guilt. You focus on the acts prohibited to god man but does not believe the fact god man commits crime less often than other criminal. Our belief gets stronger with respect to every evidence supporting to our assumption, but it is noted, belief is not rationally proportionate to evidence we came across. We try to conclude quickly or to set trend with insufficient past data, which is not rationally correct. However, our perception gets reversed while evaluating a bad guy who later on turns to be a good person. His past history of even one bad deed may require a great deal of good deeds to get his bad name wiped out. Our rationality is then struck by stubborn belief and requires disproportionate evidences to establish the fact.

Reacting to decide what is good or bad

There may be conflicting situations, wherein you may find it very difficult to understand or resorting to a particular choice whether it would end in good or it will have adverse effect on you and particularly the conflict gets worse, if other people are being affected.

Situations may vary like this:

• You are benefited but others get affected.

• You are benefited others are getting affected in short run but all are benefited in long run.

• All are getting affected in short run but all are benefited in long run.

There are many other variants of situations also, but you might have noted there are distinct parameters to consider affecting your choice of option. The distinct parameters are:

1. Qualitative view point (on quality of end result): Evaluating the outcome as how good is also a subjective judgment. However, in most of the cases, judgment can be made universal, taking opinion from others who are getting affected or seeking expertise on that matter. In case of division of inherited properties among the successors of owners, all successors can sit together to decide whether division is beneficial for all. Suggestions may be invited from other family members to cast light on it. Whatever decision is made thus can be made universally acceptable based on what end result will bring about desirable changes in all.

2. Quantitative view point: How many persons are being affected and how many persons are getting benefited are taken into consideration in this scenario. On a judgment where less no is getting affected and most are benefited is considered a rational choice. However, even if judgment is rational, all cannot be satisfied at once. Many options may be exercised for optimization to minimize loss of benefit e.g. those who are getting affected, can be provided with

other means of benefit or benefit in long run. In a case of evaluating performance appraisal and up gradation of employees in an organization, many of employees get dissatisfied. Only competent employees should get benefit, to promote overall improvement of performance of the employees. There may be some persons who cannot be promoted even if they have competency. In such cases, scale all the eligible employees on their competency and attitudes and other qualities on weighted attributes. It would be easier to decide on quantified values which are more rational, based on key attributes contributing to fulfil objectives.

3. Time line: Benefit over time line is the most difficult to evaluate. Past experience or previous reference is counted as most popular aspect for forecasting future likelihood. For example, appreciation of value of immovable properties with respect to time is almost certain. Even rate of appreciation of immovable properties in certain location is higher than the other location which depends on existing infrastructures, connectivity, amenities available and demand; therefore, time line aspect is different in various scenarios where long run and short run is being evaluated. Whenever past experience or references are formed out of short term memory, it is difficult to create better perspective view on long term future. Therefore we must understand the broader time line to consider past data of references for evaluation of trend.

4. Transparency: Since justice must also appear to have done, just as much as actually done by the judge in court of law signifies importance of transparency, judgmental rationale is part of objective of judgment. Any

independent observer should be able to see rationale behind any judgment passed on others.

Analyzing beliefs and myths

Beliefs and myths are prevalent in decision making process while only a few are willing to go up to the bottom of it for getting rid of them. Whether being rational or irrational, we may fall prey of false beliefs or myths in the following non-exhaustive circumstances of mental limits:

Not being curious enough

When somebody criticizes us, we tend to get defensive rather than to enquire how they formed the belief about us. We try first to prove ourselves before letting them (critics) to prove their point. In case, we find criticism is correct, we don't seek advice from the critics to improve.

Myth around the self belief is created whenever we don't allow any input from others about our weaknesses or people around us hide the facts about us. In such case, put yourself in the mould of critic and try to find wrong about you. You can easily find and avoid myth around self belief if you lend your ear to effective listening from others and from self as well.

Putting ego in forefront

In most cases of conflict with others, we tend to satisfy and protect our ego; still we believe that we are not the ones who are affected by our ego. Our mistaken belief about our ego affecting our decision or behaviour never allows us to see within our self. Irrationality is the best friend of ego thus it protects itself by hurting rationality very often. Being conscious about ill effects of ego, is always helpful to keep it away from such conflict between ego and cognitive behaviour.

Blindly or wrongly following the role model

We tend to follow our predecessor or role model in every aspect, not considering the fact, there may be other reason for taking that path. Suppose, your role model (an eminent person) has decided to keep his ward in convent for schooling, we may follow that as if it would also be beneficial for our child. Thus a false belief "well-proven-personal-decision-suits-to-all" is created within us. We must understand we can give our child more quality time than what our role model could have given. We must be conscious about deciding on a personalized option, which is more often a subjective choice not as universal rule to follow.

Keeping focus on short term benefit

In most of the probabilistic events, we tend to assume trend of behaviour from recent past. Even if there is periodicity over long time, we do not keep that in mind. In volatile scenario like stock market or mutual fund performance we invest based on recent past performance of the fund; long run periodicity resulted by national financial crisis, recession are grossly ignored for various reasons such as low predictability and complexity. People have short lived memory not only on memorizing past trends, but also in evaluating attributes of a person, keeping on moral path, maintaining good habits and hygiene, adopting a routine prescribed by doctor etc. Almost all of us ignore the long run benefit even if it is quite substantial, in comparison to short run benefit. We tend to choose relaxation as it gives short term comfort even if it is harmful or damaging for the future. There are several ways to avoid the bias, such as long term benefit can be translated into several tangible benefits in shorter terms for realization. It is better not to try focusing on end result but on progress to watch out.

Subjecting to inner conflict

Whenever various options are available, mind sometimes cannot settle in single decision due to lack of evaluation criteria or problem seems too complex to analyze, it goes in different directions and people get stressed. In most of cases of such indecisiveness inner conflicts plays the role. To get out of this situation rationality criteria based on probabilistic theory may be the best option to go in for. Other alternatives like heuristics short cuts may be adopted to resolve inner conflicts:

a) You may try to find a solution from other people's perspective, who are not affected by bias, consider what they would have done if they are made to choose from the alternatives you have.

b) Come up with an experimental test, in which you may choose the least preferred option and if it proves not to suit you the option may be reversed, as in case of choosing a car to buy, you may go for test drive of other cars which are not of your choice.

c) Focus on your objective not on the object, you will get better options to choose from.

d) Get rid of emotions while listing options and choosing out amongst possibilities.

What are the strategies for keeping rationale?

Quite often people get confused choosing strategies due to lack of measurable data and mental inertia due to die hard habits. Suppose, you are trying to quit smoking as per doctor's advice, since you came to know that it has potential to develop heart and lung disease. You first opt to reduce the quantity the cigarette by one piece per day. But you could not sustain your decision after 3 days. You chose another option to consume cigarette of half length keeping total no same, but could sustain the process only up to 5th day.

One of many reasons that your wish is not being fulfilled as it may be the case; you did not get any tangible benefit in short time in both cases. For quitting bad habit or to form a new habit, reinforcement by favourable outcome of positive move is required, either by realization of benefit or by decreasing trend of bad effect in concrete and measurable terms. Short term benefit may be quantified by getting an improving trend of blood pressure etc.

Even if strategies are known, implementation of the same gets affected by several factors like, procrastination due to lack of self drive, fear of failure, lack of evidences of success etc. Belief, myth and other negative forces can hinder your implementation of any good idea with little bit of uncertainty.

Various aspects on applying rationale on judgments and handling biases are discussed thoroughly in later chapters. However, the judgments based upon pure emotions or by pure logic have very limited application on day to day life. Life is much more complicated and has no one-solution-for-all problems. Practical situations are obviously a blend of events where it calls for both side of brains to act together and sometimes one requires overpowering another to achieve an optimum judgment, thereby underlines significance of visualization of positivism and optimized rationalism in all aspects.

Subjective and objective Rationality

Consider two persons having different IQ level are made to decide on single and complex solution, they have been asked to explore various alternatives on their own and told to adhere to utmost rationality in decision making process. What would happen? If rationality is objective the intelligence would not be influential upon decision making. However, in reality we observe decisions adopted are different even if all decision makers claim to have restrained within rationality. Even, it can be noted that less intelligent guy is following rational path simply because he cannot find logic in fixation of problem keeping in view persons affected or benefited by that very decision.

Consider defining rationality with respect to irrationality such that all that is not irrational is rational. In the usage of term "irrationality" is not necessarily a derogatory term nor does any decision that is not rational happen to be irrational. On the other hand the term "rational" need not be a compliment.

Rationality has to do with subjective behaviour which shall be justified, argued and adjudged universally to be truly rational. We may find that subjective rationality evokes behavioural rationality, thus we define objective rationality if the decision maker can convince arguer that he has made rational decision, while subjective rationality is established when arguer cannot convince decision maker that he has not made a rational decision.

Case-4: *Oscar Pistorus trial for Reeva Steenkamp shooting*

Six-time Paralympic gold medallist Oscar Pistorius had shot his girlfriend model Reeva Steenkamp through toilet door unknowingly to that fact that she was inside the toilet. She was shot dead in the early hours of 14th Feb 2013.

Oscar Pistorius was initially accused of culpable homicide not amounting to murder as it was assumed that he thought some intruder had entered in his room leading to his shooting for self-defence. Judge Thokozile Masipa handed down a sentence of five years in prison for Oscar Pistorius's culpable homicide charge. However, after two years, Supreme Court of appeal had found Oscar guilty of murder and gave the ruling that there was a fundamental error in judgment of Masipa as issue was not whether or not he had direct intention to kill person behind the door but whether he had foreseen possibility of death of that assumed person. In other words murder as defined by judge is unlawful and intentional killing of another person.

In assuming the nature of crime committed by Oscar (verdict given by Masipa), what could have played to give such verdict? Let us put down the possible irrationality in judgment:

a) Was she influenced by grief-stricken Oscar, who has acknowledged that he had fired through toilet door being unaware of the fact that Reeva is behind toilet? And his punishment would be injustice over his present inconsolable grief?

b) Or she was influenced by high profile accused who had been a national celebrity of South Africa and as a result whose achievement eclipsed over suspicion that he might have a wrong intention?

c) Error in judging the fine line between sets of comparatives, such as, intention to kill someone known vs. intention to kill someone unknown and shooting at someone without intent & foresight vs. shooting at someone foreseeing and ensuring the possibility of death.

d) Or she was failing to understand rationality of using firearms as self defence measure while suspected intruder is not in a position to pose any threat (from inside the toilet)?

By giving the judgment as culpable homicide the most possible reason could be that Masipa captured Oscar's intent-less killing of his wife as key pointer (as in point C) because Oscar's emotion for loss of his dear one might be highlighting his intention towards Reeva. Whereas the proceedings in lower court undermined the act of Oscar to someone unknown was supposed to be key to judgment.

Case-5: *Nobel peace prize 2013 controversy*

India's Kailash Satyarthi and Pakistan's Malala Yousafzai were awarded the Nobel Peace Prize 2014 for their great contribution towards children's education "showing great personal courage" and their struggle against the suppression of children and young people. However, Nobel Peace Prize in 2013 was much awaited for Pakistani girl Malala Yusufzai, which was awarded to UN body OPCW (organization for prohibition of chemical weapons) and evoked global criticism among the media. The reaction of the world about awarding to OPCW, was not very positive, people see reason behind the awarding OPCW, for elimination of chemical weapon stockpile by this UN body, is flimsy as it's the routine responsibility of that organization, Journalists in all round the world characterized OPCW as 'little known' and, as a 'chemical weapons watchdog'. It is true, it was too little known to be nominated for award and the Nobel Prize was meant to focus attention on this organization and its mandate.

Reason may be like this; following the US attack scenario with Syria, where chemical weapon might have used widely, could be better eliminated. On becoming the 190th member of OPCW, Syria has to follow agreement to search out and destroy all chemical weapons. Armed with this award, the organization will do better task in its prerogative.

On the other hand, the popular vote was in favour of Malala Yousufzai, who fought for the cause of women's education and nearly got assassinated by Taliban for doing so. She was shot into her head and miraculously survived. Her contribution for women's education and empowerment against all odds was recognized by rest of the world and thus nomination for the Nobel prize in 2013 was logically convincing. By giving this award to an organization whose normal routine task and denying an individual with heroic deeds proved judgment is not based upon merit. In majority of award or nomination for same, selection is not always based on pure logic and merit, rather it focused on uncommon problem fixing.

Rationale behind selection of awardees becomes different as the viewpoints taken into considerations are different among the people depending upon the people and their common perception. In order to avoid such controversies, the set of guidelines including exceptions, preferences etc may be rationally framed and displayed to observers to alleviate such controversies among people at large.

Case-6*: Excavation for hidden treasure in Unnao's Fort*

A decision taken by government in Oct 2013, to excavate fort at Daudiakala village in Unnao, once owned by former king Raja Rao Ram Bux Singh, for searching suspected hidden gold to amount thousands of tons.

Action was triggered after a seer claimed that the Raja had appeared in his dream and told him that 1,000 tonne of gold lay buried in its ruins; the Raja, was hanged in 1858 after a mutiny against the then ruler of India the Britishers.

Now the question is raised whether decision was rational, populist, and optimistic or a heuristics short cut or having any other motives hidden within. Decision based upon somebody's dream is an irrational act, however could be rationalized if evidentiary or historical data supports the proposition.

Let us analyze decision criteria with respect to have possible blend:

Is it purely optimist? It would have been said optimist if possibility of getting treasure is actually lower than assumed by gut feeling. Since there was much hoopla created before taking up excavation of the site and extensive media coverage has created the irrational optimism among the people. It was seen thousands queued up for their claim of treasure.

Rationally optimized? The decision criteria are very far from being rationally optimized. Further investigation with available technology would have helped reach a conclusion if there is any sign of buried yellow metal in this zone. These not only substantiate the presence of treasure but it can also pinpoint the location where to dig out and up to what depth. Therefore the decision lacks rationally optimized criteria.

Or a heuristic short cut? Digging up to certain location, size and depth were not based upon logic or any supportive historical data. Since they decided out of several trial and errors, it is seen the action followed heuristic short cut.

Or populist? The decision is closely following these criteria as fulfilling people's demand or supporting opinion or diverting media attention is the common strategies of political leaders which put their rationale in back seat.

While the place is of lower historical value in terms of potential to have thousand tons of gold buried underground, the decision seems to appease a large cross section of mass only. It is also evident the leaders are supporting the decision only justifying populist criteria, as going against the wind would be nothing but a politically incorrect decision.

Whatever be the kind of situation, we may pass through, we rarely use rationality as a foremost criteria, rather we believe "choosing rationality is the most irrational thing on earth" since we believe rationalism is a difficult path; we have to be subjective to protect our own interest. Still we can do justice to 'rationality' so as to honour the compliment of human being as 'most rational animal'. It is possible if we opt out of hardcore rationalist path to embrace more practicable principles of optimal rationality.

CHAPTER-4

Determinism, randomness and free will

"Which do you think is more valuable to humanity?

a. Finding ways to tell humans that they have free will despite the incontrovertible fact that their actions are completely dictated by the laws of physics as instantiated in our bodies, brains and environments? That is, engaging in the honored philosophical practice of showing that our notion of "free will" can be compatible with determinism?

or

b. Telling people, based on our scientific knowledge of physics, neurology, and behavior, that our actions are predetermined rather than dictated by some ghost in our brains, and then sussing out the consequences of that conclusion and applying them to society?

Of course my answer is b)." **-Jerry A. Coyne**

"Extremely unlikely events occur every moment and it is not a priori unthinkable that the evolution of life should be due to mere chance than that a particular order in a pack of cards should result from mechanical shuffling." – **Leszek Kolakowski**

"Has entire creation of the universe resulted out of mere coincidence or happened as a predetermined order?" This question strikes in minds of most of us. Looking at beginning of creation, just a moment before BB (big bang), space time remained in absolute singularity and it is quite impossible to predict at that very moment what is going to happen next. We are equally unable to predict what went before the absolute singularity coming into existence. The time started ticking just after BB with the expanding universe and at that moment (in present times as well) it is still remain unpredictable when the world would stop expanding. Consider evolution of galaxies and planetary systems, are they following a particular order or they are created and will run out of fuel by chance? Can we predict something which has not yet occurred so far or even a zero probable event like starburst or death of a star can be predicted so well? The question "whether natural events including creation of universe is deterministic or purely happened by chance?" remained unanswered in present time and happening of existing physical world remained mostly inexplicable.

When we talk about determinism it reminds us the probability of happening things in future ascertained on the basis of frequency of events occurred in the past. "Randomness" is truly opposite to determinism, which suggests it is not at all predictable whether or not caused by any known event. Random events are not biased by anything and cannot be influenced by anyone to make the favourable thing happen. The question is pertinent whether this determinism or randomness is equally applicable to social science. It is worthwhile to ask whether our world is truly deterministic or more blatantly we can ask whether all past events are true representative of events which would happen in future. In the domain of probability and natural science causal or material determinism (the doctrine that believes everything is caused by prior conditions, making the future events impossible to alter), holds the principle of determining the future by knowledge of exact location and the velocities of each interacting particles. According to Heisenberg uncertainty principle, position and momentum of every interacting particle cannot be known with equal accuracy. The more precise location of particle is predicted the less accuracy of momentum of the same is obtained. According to this view our real quantum universe is not precisely predictable. Whether or not probability is applicable to it, we use the theorem when we do not have enough information or sufficient calculation capabilities. This gives rise to idea of principle of indifference which is generally attributed to Jacob Bernoulli (sometimes to Laplace). In simple sense, the principle of indifference, also known as the principle of insufficient reason suggests that if there are 'n' possible outcomes, and if there is no reason to view or have insufficient information about varied likelihood, as one event is more likely than another, then each should be assigned a probability of 1/n. However, this principle has to be applied with great care, as by human nature we may turn blind eye to hidden complexity of nature and always like to find easy path to move on.

Suppose you are made to answer the following probabilistic events:

Q1. What is the probability of picking up queen of hearts from a pack of cards?

Q2. You decide to travel 100KM by road, what is probability that you would find a level crossing with rail gate closed?

Q3. What is the probability that I will survive up to 90?

Q4. What is the probability of third world war would begin in next 10 years?

Q5. What is the probability that stock market will crash next year?

Q6. What is the probability that sun will not rise from tomorrow onwards?

Just try to solve the questions with classical probability approach you will find it easier to solve Q1, Q2 being a bit harder and whereas Q3, Q4 and Q5, especially Q4 and Q5 are more difficult to solve as more uncertainty is involved due to subjective behaviour of large population. The characteristic of the masses depends on the predictability of subjective behaviour of individual. The individual sometimes behaves as per his own will, but most of the times influenced by other factor or factors or even by behaviour of masses. Therefore, we need to clarify the concept of "freewill" which forms the basis of classical approach to probabilistic behaviour of individual.

Wikipedia defines "Free will" as the ability to choose between different possible courses of action. It is closely linked to the concepts of responsibility and other judgmental parameters which apply only to actions that are freely chosen. Now, we have to find answer of this question whether we have free will or not. We know majority of us impeded by factors or constraints like metaphysical (theological, nomological), physical, social constraints like belief, religious rituals, censure, mental or psychological compulsions like phobias, neurological disorders, genetic predisposition, which affect our decision making process. It is true that humans have a strong sense of freedom, which compels us to believe that we have free will. This intuitive feeling of free will is mistaken when we are made to choose from options and we do not make a conscious decision avoiding constraints. It is very difficult to foreclose the intuitive influence that affects our conscious decisions. Even if we have free will (means our decision are free from all such constraints and we are free to choose any option from available alternatives), can this free will be predicted. Consider this example:

What is the probability that I will met a road accident while going to Delhi from Shahjahanpur covering a distance of 350KM driving alone?

Can we predict the probability by taking all past driving experiences and skill of mine and behaviour of all drivers into consideration? Keeping the fact in view, skill of assessing other drivers while negotiating traffic is the next major factor that comes after driving skill of mine. The prediction of probabilities become less complex when we consider similar facts with driving similar stretches ruling out behaviour of other drivers by generalization or averaging the skill of drivers.

Now consider another event: What is the probability of keeping a Rs 1000 note unpicked by busy road side for 24 hours?

The problem encounters the behaviour of others persons only who are not in my control but the behaviour of mine is non-influential on others. Even if individuals have free will it is very safe to predict that it won't be remaining in its position after 24 hours as any person who is picking up the note can exercise his free will while picking up the same. Here we may predict true behaviour of human and we can safely generalize the predicted behaviour for large cross section of mass. Therefore, subjective experience of free will does not contradict prediction of human behaviour at large.

Now consider answering the last question. It is much more difficult to predict occurrence of an event which has not yet occurred in the past, but still occurrence is probable in future. Mathematical calculation falls short to define such non-zero probability. However if we see the cosmic events, happenings of non-zero probable events are in abundance. Creation of universe since BB (big bang), creation of earth, creation of lives on earth had not only been unpredictable, but the probability of those events would have been very close to zero. Many events in the present world like finding a friend in face book or wining a lottery or catching a fish in a river with fishing rod have the chances of one in million or so, but it happens. It is because of the fact friends are sending requests to connect, someone has to win the lottery, and fishes are attracted to fish food attached to anchors. Most of the terrestrial events happening day to day are not truly random in nature.

Consistency of determinism with free will

Going through the conventional taxonomy of determinism and free will in the realm of philosophy we can derive the four terms as under:

	Free will is impossible	Free will is possible
Physical determinism exists	Hard determinism	Compatibilism
Physical determinism does not exist	Hard incompatiblism	Libertarianism

Hard determinists believe people are like highly complex molecular machines who find determinism is true and incompatible with notion of free will, therefore, they believe that people are devoid of free will.

Hard incompatibilism states that physical world does not follow in deterministic way, i.e. Past events are not truly representative of future events. It does not believe either that free will is possible.

Compatibilists believe physical world is deterministic and believe in existence of free will. Therefore they believe determinism is compatible with free will. A few even holds that determinism is necessary for existence of free will, arguing that choice of options requires preference for one course of action over another, which can be resulted out of past experience of similar event.

Libertarians claim that determinism in physical does not exist however free will is at least possible.

The Arguments

Taxonomy of Free will and determinism was based upon different views of the philosophers; although arguments supporting each notion are inconclusive, but interaction of human behaviour with physical events can be well understood. There is a traditional argument on doctrine of incompatibilism which highlights that a person is having free will if he is like other mechanical things such as windup toys, robots etc that are determined in their behaviour. This reasoning has been rejected by compatibilists on the grounds that, humans can be different than these objects even if human has something in common with these things.

Most incompatibilists argue that a person's freedom of action not only consists of his voluntary action but also he must be having single, originating and ultimate authority for causing his actions, thereby shows his free will. A person being responsible for his choices is the first cause, i.e. it is not resultant of any other antecedent cause. Therefore the argument illustrates, if man has free will, then man is the ultimate cause of his actions. On the other hand if determinism exists, then all of man's choices are caused by events outside his control. On reverse, if every action a person takes if caused by external factors outside his control, then he has no ultimate authority to the cause of his actions, thus he has no free will.

In the 1960s Carl Ginethe has introduced another argument called consequence argument which runs along like this: if determinism exists, then we have no control over past events that determined our present and no control over the laws of nature. Since we cannot exercise control over these, the consequences of the same is out of our control. Abiding by the principle of determinism our present choices and actions, are the consequences of the past and the laws of nature, therefore, we have no control over present; thus, no free will is possible.

This argument poses difficulties to compatibilist to encompass all actions one can be free to choose from the choices other than he or she has committed. Suppose, a compatibilist has dropped a glass wilfully on the floor that caused glass to break into pieces. The other moment he may say he could have held the glass in his hand. Going with the consequence argument, it can be explained if he held the glass instead of dropping, he either would have violated the law of the nature or have changed the past. Therefore choice of any action other than committed one becomes an imaginary event.

Problem with hard determinism

The fact is that hard determinism never allows any room for hope, effort and it leads to feeling of helplessness and pessimism. Moreover it does not support well the principle of survival of the fittest in evolution of species, as individual effort would be lost in pursuit of survival if hope does not exist. In order to bridge the arguments William James coined the term "soft determinist" and he argued against hard determinism, emphasizing that the important issue is not personal responsibility and authority of decider, but hope. He proposed the way to allow a role for chance without having belief in existence of free will.

In fact, "soft determinism" is more acceptable notion of philosophy as hard determinism is losing ground since it cannot explain most of the facts of metaphysical world. In Biological determinism, as it holds good in biology, heredity and reproduction underlines natural selection which gets along with factor of chance. Millions of sperms are required for impregnation, however only one is sufficient for the action, so that only healthiest sperm can succeed. The nature has given everything in abundance so as to happen the most desirable outcome.

Whether or not the creation of universe follows determinism, it does not change the fact that the future of event outside scientific determinism will be mostly unknown and will always be. Therefore, such an event in future can be presented as a chance out of possible outcomes.

Now the question whether there lies any fallacy among determinism of events, happening by chance and existence of free will, even whether these are mutually exclusive to each other. Let us analyze events that mathematically probable but physically improbable.

Suppose you hit the billiard balls and the balls forms various irregular shapes after getting first hit and stopped at different locations. On several trials various shapes are formed. Suppose you are to find, what will be the probability of forming a square shape after first hit, it may be mathematically possible as it may require infinite no of trial, however it may be concluded from intuition as well as data of past events, that it is a physically improbable event to occur.

Consider another natural event, suppose you would like see your name written in English by formation of cloud hovering in the sky. Although it is mathematically possible but is physically improbable.

In both the cases, it is contrary to natural law. Even if the first case being very much subjective, any hit on the billiard ball cannot cause such regular shape as natural law indicates forming an irregular and random shape after single hit. Any options exercised by any person having free will cannot cause that event. Therefore, presence of free will does not suffice to cause an outcome when events are following randomized behaviour.

Now consider you would like to hit two sixes per over by pull shot in a limited over cricket. The opportunity of hitting a pull shot is created by bowler but hitting over the boundary depends on how and at what impact you can give the ball a perfect hit. Here the future is collectively dependent on bowler as well as on your batting skill. Here your free will and randomness (for the time being facing a bowler may be assumed as random event) both co-exist.

If you see the natural events, such as procreation, it would remind us creating more possibilities towards desirable outcomes. Flowers get pollinated, plants bear fruits, seeds are spread naturally through birds, animals; the fact renders maximum possibilities to generate progeny and spreading the species to get even nutrition to live on. Even in animals millions sperms are generated while only one is required for procreation. Therefore the nature accepts randomness of events and does not depend upon predeterminism or destiny which is believed by human. Therefore all facts are inexplicable by determinism.

Even if biological determinism exists in genetic predisposition, replicating physical and emotional attributes in heredity, it is physically possible to choose sex of offspring exercising your free will in the domain of determinism. With the development of medical science you can inject stem cell leaving it to initiate healing process on its own; thereby you exercise biological determinism in the domain of free will.

Even if causal determinism exists in certain events in the nature, randomness also co-exists. It is not well predicted by natural creature whether occurring any event requires any cause or not and the nature has endorsed it.

The arguments on free will is also equally never ending, however, it is also a fact existence of the same in absolute sense is questionable and the notion believing free will not helping us to avoid prejudices, false belief, myths, intuition and ill effects of undue influences on our decision making processes.

Swami Vivekananda offered good understanding of free will who stated that the will was not "free" because it was heavily influenced by the law of cause and effect—"The will is not free, it is a phenomenon bound by cause and effect, but there is something behind the will which is free." Swamiji never emphasized determinism of universal events and past karma of individuals instead he showed that honest endeavour can change one's future. He said "It is the coward and the fool who says this is his fate. But it is the strong man who stands up and says I will make my own fate"

If we believe in existence of determinism in macroscopic events of the universe, probably we are binding ourselves to the biased belief that there is no scope of randomness in colossal universe. Even if causal determinism exists in all events we are unable to unearth every underlying cause-effect relationship either and we have to resort to randomness, intuitive possibilities and calculative probabilities. In order to win a lottery (believed to be the effect of determinism) we have to exercise our will to buy a ticket. We have to take part to win a race. Although we are unable to detect every reason behind the outcome factors affecting the likelihood of occurrence can be known from past events where we can exercise our free will improving possibilities to happen the desired outcome.

Principle of indifference and physical world

It is generally accepted that the physical laws governing in a macroscopic system are not enough understood to predict every outcome within it. More often, it is not practically feasible to device certain process to discover underlying cause and action to get precise output as per our choice. It is understood that given sufficient time and resources, suitable precise measurements could not be made, by which we can predict the outcome of coins, dice, and cards with high accuracy. In case of flipping a coin, initial momentum can cause the outcome to happen but momentum imparted to the coin during its launch is not known with sufficient accuracy, thereby we are compelled to explain outcomes as random events.

Our inability to detect or measure the causes has given rise to idea of principle of indifference, which is focused on the exploring the mutually exclusive and collectively exhaustive possibilities. The principle states that if there 'n' nos. of exhaustive and mutually possibilities exist, then each possibility should be assigned an equal probability ie. 1/n. The rule also asserts that if there is no known reason for relating the problem to several alternatives, then relatively to such knowledge the assumptions of each alternative have an equal probability. For example, if there is no known reason for saying a ball is yellow rather than red then, relative to this knowledge, ball being yellow and red becomes equi-probable.

It is very well understood that our limited knowledge can misuse this principle to explain all possible events. Any problem which is ill-posed leads to contradiction and subjective error and unique solution cannot be arrived at. This principle, as it stands, very often lead to paradoxical and even contradictory conclusions.

Let us assume a proposition which does not have any relevant external evidence, Q and let Q' be the contradictory of Q.

Assume we have no reason to favour Q or Q'

By the Principle of Indifference, p(Q)= p(Q'). It follows p(Q)=p(Q')=1/2 as p(Q)+p(Q')=1 (Sum of all possibilities=1)

Let us analyze an example in two aspects.

Approach-1 (ratio)

Suppose you are to flip three coins one by one.

The exhaustive possibilities as per ratio approach are:

1. One head and two tail

2. Two head and one tail

3. Three head

4. Three tail

Each of above possibilities have one fourth (1/4) equal probabilities.

Approach-2 (Flip by flip)

In flip by flip approach the possibilities are:

1. First coin head, second and third coin tail

2. First and second coin head, third coin tail

3. First and third coin head, second coin tail

4. First coin tail, second and third coin head

5. First and second coin tail, third coin head

6. First and third coin tail, second coin head

7. First, second, third coin head

8. First, second, third coin tail

We get eight possibilities each having equal probabilities of one eighth. Therefore, two approaches have indicated different probability of identical possibility as seen in Sl 3 and 4 of approach-1 & 7 and 8 of approach-2. Therefore it appears to have refuted the principle of indifference.

If we once again give a closer look to approach-1, we may note that possibility 1 and possibility 2 are having different probabilities than that of 3 and 4, as 1 or 2 are having 3 times as much probable as 3 or 4. Therefore, the principle of indifference has apparently been falsified as the problem is wrongly approached. If we consider there is no ignorance or lack of knowledge lie beneath our assumption of possibilities, then our knowledge about one possibility does not affect change of probability of another.

Let us prove that we have ignorance in presenting problem in ratio approach.

p(first coin head) =1/4 (possibility 4) +1/12(possibility1/3) + 2/12 (possibility2/1.5) =1/2

Similar way, p(first coin tail)=1/2p(second and third coin head)=1/4(possibility4)+1/12(possibility2/3)=1/3

Now as per Baysian probability theorem, probability of first coin appears head learning that second and third coin appear head,

P (first head| second & third head)= P(first head, second & third head)/ P(second third head)=(1/4)/(1/3)=3/4

Whereas p (first coin head) was derived as per ratio approach was 1/4 has been raised, which was happened due to our ignorance.

One such example existed through more than hundred years. Joseph Louis Bertrand, a French mathematician introduced a probability problem in nineteenth century which is now known as Bertrand's paradox, implies principle of indifference is not applicable to find probability of events having infinite random possibilities. He cited an example "We trace at random a chord in a circle. What is the probability that it would be smaller than the side of the inscribed equilateral triangle?"

We obtain three different answers if principle of indifference in three different approaches for constructing the chord:

a) If the chords are constructed parallel to one of the sides, and if they lie within inner side of radius perpendicular to them, then the probability is one-half (refer: FIG-A).

b) If the chords are drawn from vertex of the inscribed triangle up to the circumference at opposite side, the longer than side of the triangle fall within the angle

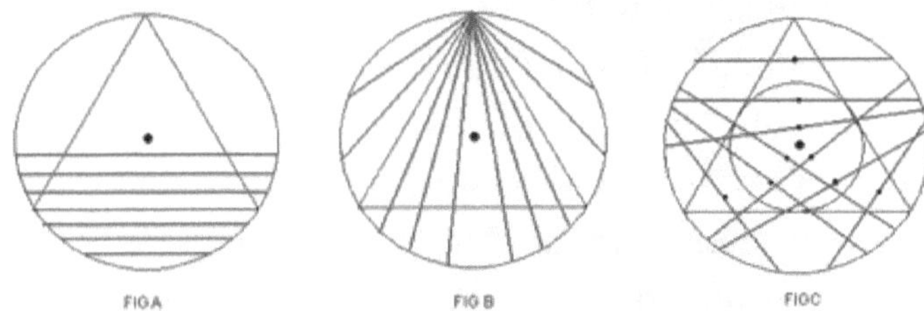

formed by two adjacent sides of the vertex, the probability of longer chords become two third, thus probability of chord being smaller will be one third (refer: FIG-B).

c) If the chord drawn like this so that its midpoint falls within a circle inscribed the triangle so that larger than side of triangle is produced. Then the probability of chord being longer than side of triangle will be one fourth as area of circle inscribing the triangle is one fourth against the outer circle, Then the chord being smaller than side of the triangle becomes three fourth (refer: FIG-C).

Although it may seem that Bertrand's paradox signifies failure of principle of indifference however, it emphasized failure of our epistemic capacities. John Maynard Keynes stated that "The perceptions of some relations of probability may be outside the powers of some or all of us".

He concluded. "So long as we are careful to enunciate the alternatives in a form to which the Principle of Indifference can be applied unambiguously, we shall be prevented from confusing together distinct problems, and shall be able to reach conclusions in geometrical probability which are unambiguously valid"

Nicholas Shackel in his paper "Bertrand's Paradox and the Principle of Indifference" stated that "The difficulties we have in getting knowledge of transfinite objects leaves us ignorant of the intrinsic structure of many such objects. Most philosophers of probability who want to make use of the principle of indifference think that probabilities are internally related to rational degrees of belief and, for that reason, are unlikely to think that the principle of indifference is a purely metaphysical principle."

How do we relate real life?

In real life scenario we get easily bogged down with complexities of decision making criteria. No matter how complex is the mixture, the situation can be analyzed to arrive at a solution. Let's discuss how to simplify:

1. Events not yet occurred and have no history of similar occurrence, but always have chance to occur (non-zero probable event like death of star): It is broadly unpredictable due to insufficient data available. It is deterministic in nature and may turn to predicable if data is made available. In order to enhance predictability,

means to probe into similar events may be employed (pl refer Apollo Moon Mission in Chapter-1).

2. A few events characterize trials with limited outcomes (like throwing dice): Each outcome is random and unpredictable but large sample size collectively follows certain probability distribution which is predictable and outcome can be utilized. In order to make the favourable outcome appear, repeat several times or make the total no of event larger.

3. Events influenced by subjectivity: It may appear as unpredictable, but due to generalized nature of human being it can be predictable (e.g. probability of being 1000 rupee note left unpicked beside a busy road).

4. Reactive human behaviour: It is deterministic (biological) broadly. Presence of free will may co-exist if choices are having similar outcomes.

5. In physical world randomness and determinism always co-exist, irrespective of what compatibilist or incompatibilist opines about. Just remember, most of the major terrestrial events (non-zero events which has never been occurred) are unpredictable and may be considered random, however, day to day events (day, night, seasons) are deterministic. The natural calamities are still broadly unpredictable (a few events like cyclone, thunder storm etc. gives us time to raise alarm). Earth quake, Tsunami, effect of global warming remained as unpredictable as data are inadequate for prediction, therefore these events may be treated as random events.

6. Majority of life problems are a blend between two parameters: randomness (outcome is causeless or

dependent on others beyond our control) and determinism (having cause-effect relationship). Outcomes totally dependent on subjective decisions are deterministic. As discussed in Chapter-1 (under subjectivity of visualization), subjective elements can be segregated out to exercise control over it. Outcomes of random nature can only be maximized to make it happen.

7. We have free will to adopt suitable process explaining nature of outcome and we can challenge most of the life problems by exercising our free will while choosing out most suitable choice for maximizing possibilities.

8. The principle of indifference explains most of the natural and real life phenomena so long as we can well pose the problem. In case, the problem is much complex for analyzing and benefit at the end is insignificant, we may adopt the principle of indifference.

CHAPTER-5

The way to look at things

"Once we open our eyes to the infinite magic that the universe has in abundance, we are sure to be enthralled by what we see and this miraculous creation gets us closer to our dreams and to the world as a whole."-**Stephen Richard**

"Anything at all is possible. Some things are unlikely. Some things will never happen. But they always could, at any time." -**Ashly Lorenzana**

"In practical life we are compelled to follow what is most probable; in speculative thought we are compelled to follow truth."-**Baruch Spinoza**

Recently, I came across a blog authored by Bari Bardhan regarding 'intelligent people struggle to succeed'. He believes that personal success depends on factors, out of which intelligence is one. And he wrote "I was never formally identified as a "gifted" child, but there were many salient indications that I was much further ahead on the IQ curve than my peers (e.g. reading at a much earlier age, skipping a grade, etc.). This led to a great deal of external pressure from family, friends and those who had a stake in my success (teachers, principal, etc.)."

Indeed, too much optimism about anything or anybody can put pressure on the subject that leads to struggle for success. It may also lead to positivity bias, which is nothing but a bias against negativity rather than a tool for optimism.

For this bias we forget the unpleasant or the negative instances or incidents happened to our life. Is that what we think positivism ought to be?

On the flip side it is termed as, "emotional alignment for seeing things in optimistic way, connecting to positive things happened in the past". This effect also pertains to the tendency of people, especially when they evaluate the causes of the behaviours of a person they like, to attribute the person's inherent character as the cause of their positive behaviours. Generally, as people grow older, they tend to look to the past in positive light. In comparison to younger adults' memories, older adults' memories are more likely to consist of positive memories than negative one. Positive mind set is essentially required to boost up the process of sustenance and growth.

As we observed in physical world, nature of occurrence of events are difficult to be defined on purely deterministic approach nor they are truly random so that probability approach can be directly applied, this insufficiency has led to principle of indifference, also known as the principle of insufficient reason. This practical probabilistic approach bridges between our emotional attribute and logical arguments in defining the events and outcomes resulting in balancing act of logical and emotional brain. Between the viewpoints of uncertainty and determinism there lies the hope which is evolved from positivism of human mind.

Concoction of ideas that tries to randomize natural events with optimism can lead to positivism which effectively blends the positive emotional attributes with probability of happening things to achieve optimized reasonability in a bid to shape the future rather than only predicting it.

Are possibilities always misunderstood?

How frequent are the events which occur with improbable possibilities? It is contrary to our general belief that in most cases improbable possibilities do occur. If we look deep into the problem, it may be seen most of the cosmic events have infinite possibilities and going with the principle of indifference, every possibility has infinitesimal probability (value closer to zero). Therefore, each possible alternative seems not to happen, however a single possibility out of countless ones must occur which is also having infinitesimal probability, and thus most often improbable probability happens.

Sometimes, in the event with observable large and finite possibilities, a few possibilities are wrongly assumed to be improbable due to our lack of knowledge to explore exhaustive alternatives. Reverse is also evident in our real world, happening things in future seems to be unpredictable as either number of possibilities conceived are countless or has ulterior influence over each other which goes undetectable.

Nevertheless, we try to find optimistic alternative among countless such dark physical possibilities even if most of them goes beyond our expectation. The optimistic realization of someone's expectation gives rise to positive visualization.

Whenever we look into future, we tend to see ourselves in a position which is either better or worse than that existing situation which depends upon our type of past experiences, interaction between logical and intuitive mind and reactive output of cognitive and emotional brain. We may be able to categorize all future outcomes, through logical approach, classified into two broad outcomes; one is positive or optimistic outcomes, the other is negative or pessimistic outcomes. Nevertheless, we tend to pick out most expected outcomes through intuitive approach. Positive visualization mostly helps to attain desirable achievement in less painful way ignoring obstacles and hurdles coming on your way, but sometimes it debilitates energy by way of enjoying virtual fruits of success much earlier than actual achievement. Sometimes even positive visualization leads to contentment disregarding hard work involved in achieving goal, therefore it calls for justified approach to utilize positive visualization in certain places.

On the other hand, rational approach to visualization lies on logical path wherein every action is dependent on reality and evidences. Purely rational path is the hardest of all, as decision making process gets complex with handling numerous inputs and anybody may find himself bogged down to frustration handling numerous data and analysis of the same. However, the rational visualization can further be optimized with positivism combining thought processes of both side of brain, which may be called optimally rational visualization. It is to ensure realistic view of future having optimized outcome making it more likely to happen. As we came to know from the recent scientific experiments about left and right side of brain and interaction between the both, we must use our full potential of objectivity wherever it is required to make the possibilities brighter. Positive and rational visualization can be treated as both side of coin, by which you are able to confine your approach in right direction ensuring your expectation not harmed by negative expectation as well as keeping your energy level up for overcoming obstacles.

To look at in normative approach

Visualization starts with observation which is considered to be the most important tools for taking inputs from the environment. The more you see the more you believe and the more likely to get the desired input. In each object in a particular event has got minute details and has infinite depth to see, but it is the observer who has to decide up to what extent observation is made to order to make it purposeful.

Robert Wolf, Chief Executive Officer of UBS Americas, Inc. said "observation is a process of immersing oneself in listening and looking more carefully, without judging, without letting thought intrude between observer and the object. If you see a beautiful landscape and utter "how beautiful" you might have missed full of it and seen what may otherwise you can see. There is lot of difference between seeing vs. looking at."

Consider you are in a strange place where you are trying hard to find a public phone booth to make a call.

Ultimately you find one and there incidentally meet a friend who is searching hard for a post office. He asks if you have come across any post office in this region. You run your thought back ward down the recent memory whether you have seen one. But you can't recollect anything as you had turned your eyes on to watch a call booth not for post office. Wonder how this could be? It is because you've turned on left brain and left it open to accept-reject mode. Your eyes had collected each snapshot and sent the signal to brain to analyze whether it is call booth or not. Your brain said 'no' until you have found one and confirmed as 'yes'. During that time right brain was not activated to see what it was; if it was not call booth, no input was recorded in the recent memory.

Ideal observation must be free from prejudice and preconceived belief which may block your vision for picking up required information. However, every observation has its depth up to which someone has to reach for. If you want every cue to be at your disposal, you have to activate both left and right side of the brain. And you cannot straight way make your left or right side brain activated at your will, rather you have to initiate process so as to brain conceives which part to activate.

Let us start with key parameters of observation:

Resemblance: Human tendency is to tag every object with resemblance with another object. Another object may lie in the viewer's memories of the past related to similar or unrelated events. The habit of finding resemblance can be useful to attach visual tag to object you see and remember in future.

Proportionism: Any object you see gives you visual cue about its true behaviour, even if it is faking to appear something different, it would obviously tell about the proportion between its true and falsified presence. Anyone can spot the disproportionate attributes in character or object according to his past reservoir of memories, even a child can distinguish disproportionate behaviour of parents.

Oddity: Abnormality or oddity is the height of proportionism, where you are more likely to spot it with accuracy. Finding odd man out is more like reasoning test requiring knowledge of array of characteristics in objects in its proper place.

Character: The composition of any scene is made of characters or inanimate objects playing their individual role in a particular scenario. An observer is to see whether the scene has natural composition or faked or doctored. Natural composition underlines definite symptoms congruent to nature.

Count: The natural composition of any scene definitely tells about the numbers; any missed or absent and even any characters in excess to the scene. Observer with keen eyes can detect the same to decide compatibility with natural composition.

Finding Possibilities

We can have blind faith on probabilistic nature of happening events and rest assured letting every events emerge whatever way they can happen and justify ourselves for not putting our best efforts. On the other extreme we can also set ourselves fit for situation walking through the right path and improvising our skills continually to make things happen as per our wish.

In "Rich dad Poor dad" author Robert Kiyosaki said, rich dad always tries to find out means to overcome difficulties saying like this "I have four children, I have to be rich for their better upbringing"

Poor dad always tries to justify his inactions "I have four children, that is why I became poor"

Rich dad sees the bright side and he is able to analyze what he is ought to be and tries to get right option out of many which he explores.

Poor dad only blames it on fate; he is not able to think of any option.

Possibility thinking is essentially the most important trait of an optimist that is why they are not only able to create options but also sees the right option to choose. When we are to decide what is possible and what is not, we decide by our brain which dictates us to protect from uncertainty and letting us to choose inaction. But if we see to its depth, it is well understood, that our decisions are based on our perception and mental comfort, but obviously not perfectly based upon the real pictures of mind.

Now consider four pictures of Mobious strip (fig-1, Fig2 and Fig3, Fig4) below. (Mobious strip was originally invented by German mathematician August F Mobius in 1858) consists of single surface with both sides. It is formed by giving a rectangular strip a half twist (180 deg) and then by joining the ends together. If the strip is split along the middle of the width, the outcome will be astonishing and confusing as to find out what is possible and what is not.

Let us analyze the two set of figures with respect to possibilities:

<u>Fig-1 and Fig2</u>

<u>Fig-3 and Fig4</u>

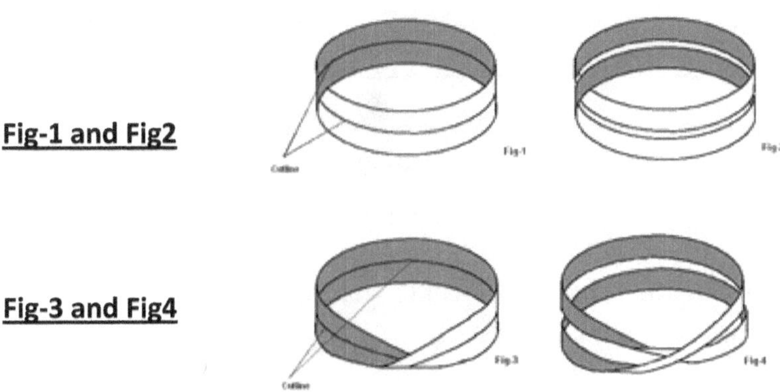

What seems impossible but actually possible	What is really impossible
Physical Construction of surface which has neither inside nor outside	Splitting into two rings by cutting along cut line at middle of width
Marking cut line with single stroke in both side	Colouring two side with two different colours

What Seems impossible but actually possible	What is really impossible
Splitting two rings each of which remains locked into another (ref fig2)	Separating two rings
Colouring 2 sides with 2 different colour	

The above example is illustrated to give an idea about differences in our assumption and the reality which is understood when we perfectly observe the objects or practically do it ourselves. There are certain ways to get your observation perfected.

Avoiding Selective seeing and listening

Our seeing and listening are greatly influenced by our previous experiences, that is why we always try to correlate facts and figures of present with the events of the past and eventually we miss important cue lies in the present. Selective seeing or taking other sensory input is the greatest barrier to perfect observation of objects around us.

Whenever you want to see or listen it must be without any preoccupation and biases in mind as several important cues are missed if you try to put your mind over processes rather than objects. The orientation of mind should be free from all such distractions.

Avoiding Pride and Prejudice

Mastering the art of observation requires letting in sights, sounds and smells without any judgment and prejudice. The experiences we gather should be focused on way of rationalizing and organizing not on finding reason behind or to establish cause-effect relationship; we should be able to develop understanding about distinct difference between seeing, knowing and telling. We have the inherent tendency to associate prejudice with experiences of outer world and to take it towards inner self. The more we get rid of the pride and prejudice, the more we can get from the surrounding without any hesitation and rejection from inner self and the more rational visualization is achieved.

Organizing memory inputs and Usage

Our eyes and other sensory organs act as interface between outer world and our brain. When we see any object, our eyes translate the visual image to signal adapting to understanding of brain. During processing the image or any inputs like smell, taste etc, electrical pulses are generated in optical sensory nerves according to what we see, more specifically what we focus and perceive the understanding of the input. Understanding of inputs depends on what we believe this information to be important for usage. For example, if we see an wild animal from very close distance, our brain process very fast whether there is any danger under way, if past memory confirms, it generates alarm by giving motor nerve a signal to strengthen for preparing ourselves for fight or flight situation. Each and every input fed is processed and stored for future usage depending upon its usability based on perception. Here lies the importance of pre-processing the inputs for better storage, in a way that stored inputs could be retrieved easily for usage.

If brain perceives any information which is important for survival or any basic need it stores the information for very long time. It is just like we do not forget hissing sound of a venomous snake even if we have heard once in our lifetime. It is thus important to know the objectives and the key inputs to make our brain understand what is meant for storage and what to forget. Therefore seeing to the bottom of the objects and feeling the parameters like shape, colour, texture, even taste, and smell and so on to its depth help making better long-time storage. The habits of seeing the objects will surely help reach your subconscious mind and can be stored in safe custody of your memory bank for disposal over and over again. The duration of storage of key observation in brain depends mainly on the following:

• The more sensory organs participated for collecting the input the more likely it remains for long. If the object's multiple visual parameters such as color, shape, orientation, time are observed, it will likely to stay longer in your memory.

• Repetition: Repetitive observation helps to recollect it more precisely.

• Sequence: Data stored sequentially will produce precise recollection. Since raw data in nature is not sequential, it is required to make sequential suitable for storage.

To see what you would love to

It is equally important to ascertain where we would like to see ourselves or what we like to see there. May be it is not visually clear, but somehow we have to draw an outline in order to fill in colour. Just recall the picture of elephant illustrated earlier in this book, even if all details are not known still we can draw the outline. We then fill in colours and firm outlines to see the output; again we may erase and refill with different tone to see whether it is matching exactly with our imagination. If it is still not clear we enlist the objectives. Clearer the objectives, more vivid are the outlines.

Suppose by closing your eyes, you would like to draw a mental picture of luxury villa which you desire to have it (no matter how much costly it is and your wealth is sufficient to buy it or not). Quite naturally, you would see the exterior first, for approaching near to main gate you obviously get down from the limousine or any other luxury car. You walk down, the guard salutes, enter the hall where interiors are draped with lavish upholstery, chandelier and other elaborative decors.

Up to this you may think of whether this mansion is double storied or not. How many rooms your house should have? Who are the others staying with you- your wife, and children, servants, drivers and cooks? Now you may imagine the house requires being large or double-storied to house a grand stair-case, many rooms with many views, servant quarters at the outhouse, a grand parking for your limo and a pool aside. You may see the colour of the interior paint, the colour of turban of the guard, the colour of curtains, the window pane, the view through it and other details.

Until getting the vivid picture, you may go back and forth iterating the objectives and required objects and underlying details. Let your imagination spread the wings and every minute details would come true its life.

To get into it whatever you love to do

You would like to love what you like to have. Love is one of the most powerful positive energies having the potential of transforming gloom into glitter, doom into dazzle. Love shall necessarily be unconditional, unprecedented to protect your dream from falling into cliff of despair. Therefore the picture of dream must be perfect and permanent, should not be faded with ravages of time and vagaries of daily life. Your love should be so strong that you have to nurture with this without any alteration to it. The nurturing requires motivation from inner self or from the surroundings, pressure from the peer group, society. Thus to get motivation from the outer world, you have to speak out your dream and about your destination. The law of nature will set the stage for you and will make the approach road leading to it, removing the hindering objects, kindling the flame of desire. Your peer group may poke you, remind you, throwing sarcastic remarks on your face, and criticize you at your back. But you will realize chasing any dream, requires inward focus, quality time to assess, monitoring activities of self and efforts required for getting rid of all insipid matter relates to whosoever around. Sometimes it may seem becoming selfish to be dream-driven, but the objectivity of the goal will tell you it will benefit others at large.

At this point, we came to understand happening in real world is blend of determinism, probabilism (absence of certainty) and a bit of free will. In this complexity, it is a matter of debate that everywhere we should keep our optimism fly high or to choose a different path optimizing various aspect. Let's go into optimization of pleasure with pain.

'Optimize Pleasure with pain'

Positivism is linked with pleasure and relaxation that is why height of positivism attracts inaction which in turn invites indulgence to fantasy which may get you into painless virtual world of pleasure, where your positive energy gets sucked in. Exercise optimal rationality for employing your imagination and virtual pleasure about future as a driving force. Follow 'Pleasure with a pain' therapy only as it helps you maintain your drive and make you feel happy at the same time. There are positive actions like celebration over smaller achievement, travelling to strange places etc. which can give your soul food sustaining your energy. Pain, as seemed to you, is essential for making the pleasure worthy of it, emphasizing the contrast between them and enabling measuring the pleasure with the yardstick of pain. Conquering pain and achieving pleasure is a function of emotional motive force or self drive.

CHAPTER 6

Mental map of self

"Anyone can become angry-that is very easy. But to be angry with right person, to the right degree, at the right time, for the right purpose, and to right way-this is not easy" --**Aristotle**

"Your memory is a monster; you forget-it doesn't, it simply files things away. It keeps things for you, or hides things from you-and summons them to your recall with will of its own. You think you have a memory; but it has you" -**John Irving**

"The glaring contrast between seeing and looking-at the world around us is immense; it is fateful. Everything in our society seems to conspire against our inborn human gift of seeing."-**Frederick Franck**

It was beginning of October 1994. I was travelling with my parents and family on the way to a northeastern state of India. We took transit stay at Guwahati, where my father met a severe accident at about 8 PM just outside railway station nearly 200m away from the station, while he was returning from reservation counter and we were waiting for him on the platform. After a while, in our shocking astonishment, we saw him rushing towards us with a bruised face bleeding profusely from nose. We got into a sudden state of shock, got totally confused to decide what to do next, as we saw him felling unconscious on the ground the moment he saw us. We regained our strength after a short while, as we observed he had a hit on his nose and got a slit of one inch. To stop the bleed we were to rush for immediate medical help. The situation came under control after three hours when we managed to get him operated in a hospital around midnight with several stitches.

I was amused and amazed how a man of 68 survived a free fall inside a deep trench during Guwahati power failure, and his rushing with bleeding nose keeping his consciousness alive until he saw us. Was it a mere coincidence? Or his brain triggered the ultimate survival weapon to keep him conscious and made his blood gushing to the lower limbs getting them strong enough to rush for help running almost quarter of a mile and the sight of us sent the signal to his brain to shut off emergency to a state of energy conservation mode, making him fall unconscious? How did I manage to get help from the group of doctors and making them agree to operate in a shabby hospital O.T. at midnight without having an sterilized operating tools, was also nothing less than miracle. We thanked divine power to provide every possible measure at right time and right spot. The nature has made all of us, capable of sustaining this kind of emergency, where logical control of brain is overridden by the surge in emotional brain. It is also contrary to my popular belief that positive emotion may also come out as emotional surge to combat the crisis.

Very often, we see our emotions manifesting as either negative or positive reactive feelings as an outcome of inputs to our brain through sensory organs and it fairly depends on the individual perception and internal communication between certain locations inside the brain. Proactive behavioural action may also evolve out of positive emotion in the form of accumulating resource for future like filling the reservoir of good memories to create pleasure, celebrating happiness to create hope etc. The emotions essentially obviously reflect as resultant behaviours, which are consequential upon one's kits for survival, life progress, state of being etc. Emotional responses can be of three types, namely behavioural, autonomic and hormonal.

The first component consists of muscular response to brain signal received and processed by motor nerves which is initiated by external input given to brain. Autonomic emotional response acts as ultimate survival kit of the possessor. Sometimes, it requires abrupt and rapid mobilization of limbs necessitating quick surge of energy for sudden forceful movement. It is caused by autonomic responses, with an urge to save itself and oppose attack against perceived danger. Whenever this situation happens, it calls for increased heart rate, rapid blood flow to lower limb from other parts of the body to get it prepared for flight-or-fight. Hormonal responses caused by epinephrine and nor-epinephrine which helps to convert stored nutrients to convert into glucose to make it available for muscles requiring instant energy.

Mind resides inside brain!

Our body is confined or limited by the boundary called "Skin". We can see our skin, hair, nails which are interfacing with environment we live in. Our sight cannot reach beneath the skin therefore we cannot see how the actions is being performed by the muscles upon signals through motor nerves, signal received by the sensory organ, conversion of energy from food and utilization by the body for performance and growth etc. But we can visualize several action of the body; even sometimes decision given by cognitive brain can be realized. We are not always able to visualize why certain external inputs result in negative emotion or positive emotion. Even we cannot find which part of our body is capable of thinking and what is mind comprising of. Modern medical science has revealed that brain is the part of body which is capable of thinking and mind is a part of emotional brain having beliefs, perception, desires, wishes and other emotional attributes, where external inputs are conceived and it decides how to react as a resultant. Man can only intuit the existence of his mind through introspection but cannot detect its tangible form. But how is mind functioning and who is controlling? Is that Brain which has empowered various parts with certain amount of autonomy to function independently for maintaining basic needs of the body? Researcher had come across various such queries until some of the mysteries got unfolded in modern brain imaging studies.

Going back to text book of evolution by Charles Darwin-human has instinctive expression of emotions which is like animals. Facial expressions of emotions fall under instinctive responses which are unlearnt and evolved from ancestors. It consists of complex set of movements of facial muscles which is controlled by innate brain mechanism just as smile, coughing, sneezing. It is well known that a born blind person is able to smile, cough and sneeze like a normal person. Heart never stops or awaits brain's instruction as it has to pump blood to every organ responsible for sustaining life. Lungs have to suck oxygen and purge out carbon-di-oxide even if body is in deep sleep. Eyelids are to blink every now and then to prevent dry-out of eyeball. Internal organs are to perform duties like digesting food, secreting enzymes; Endocrine glands are to support growth, and to enhance power to muscles whenever required.

Other than innate brain mechanism, there exist cognitive and emotionally influenced human behaviours which are evoked by environmental and neural input. If we look at our brain, it appears like an English Wall nut which is positioned inside the skull; it has crumbled and wrinkled surface and divided into two hemispheres by a distinct visible fold. Several researches have been carried out to find the exact location in the brain for thought process, emotions and memories. Path breaking work by James Papez (1937),and Paul D. MacLean (1952) revealed that emotion evolves from part of the brain called the limbic system, which consists of major parts like amygdala, hyppocampus, thalamus, hypothalamus, fornix, mammillary body, olfactory bulb, cingulate gyrus, corpus callosum etc. Researchers around various corners of globe have found the central part of brain, called amygdala complex which has the control of patterns of emotions. Medial nucleus, a major part of amygdala receives sensory inputs like, visuals, audio, odours, etc and relay the information to forebrain and hypothalamus. Lateral/basolateral nuclei receive sensory inputs from thalamus; Primary sensory cortex and hippocampal formation project it to ventral striatrum and dorso medial nucleus of thalamus which involve in reinforcing stimuli on learnt experiences. It also sends the sensory input to central nucleaus of amygdala, which is responsible of various expressions of emotional responses.

Basal nucleaus receives inputs from lateral and basolateral nuclei and relays information to periaqueductal grey matter of mid brain.

Central nucleaus of amygdala concerns most as it is the most important part involved in expression of emotional responses against external stimuli. In several researches it showed in various species, when central nucleaus is removed from brain, fear is observed to have abolished.

Several imaging studies on human brain has shown, activity of right amygdala increased when the subject work on tasks which are unsolvable, become tense, unhappy and frustrated.

Removal of prefrontal lobes in a patient resulted in several change in personality. The subject become childish, and lost the ability to carry out plans and become unemployable.

Emotions and other reactions of sensory inputs originate from the limbic system, however, the manifestation of these may be positive or negative, which is strongly influenced by the frontal lobes. It is now well known that amygdala organizes emotional responses to all situations including which produces negative emotions like, fear, anger disgust, anxiety etc. Left cerebral hemisphere is specialized for positive and approach related emotions. It is believed pre-frontal lobes give us the experience of happiness, enjoyment, satisfaction and other positive emotions. Other important positive human attributes like ethics, honesty, and creativity are also emerging out of it. The frontal lobes and the limbic system communicate through "fronto-limbic loops" to influence our experience what it ought to be either negative or positive.

Evolution of emotional responses

Since homo sapience came into being, emotional responses (positive and negative) of human race have been going through psychosomatic and socioeconomic evolution. American social psychologist, Dr. Barbara Fredrickson, has introduced Broaden-and-build theory of positive emotions which suggests that positive emotions like enjoyment, happiness, joy, inquisitiveness etc broaden one's awareness and encourage exploratory thoughts and actions. Over time, this broadened behavioural repertoire builds skills and resources, e.g., curiosity about maps and geographical terrain, flora and fauna of a region becomes valuable navigational knowledge; interest to stranger become a supportive friendship; outdoor games becomes exercise, which eventually builds physical excellence. She observed the odd play habits in young Patas monkeys (Erythrocebuspatas) on the savannahs of West Africa. When they are being chased, they prefer to fling themselves on branches of trees, saplings, which bend and can catapult them in unexpected directions. She also noted this behaviour disappears as they grow adult. However, an adult behaves in this way only when fleeing a predator. It seems that the young monkeys are engaging themselves in pointless fun, just for the sake of it. According to her theory, their joy and happiness are creating a reserve of memories that could be used in future keeping those resources alive.

We also do react in response to external stimuli, use positive emotions from our memory-reserve, nevertheless, we sometimes think of ourselves that we should behave differently in a certain situation; we find we are emotionally overridden when our cognitive brain failed to give us right decision at right time and we commit blunders. When we calm down, reversal occurs; we can search out within ourselves what is right and what is optimal. What possibly has been indicated about subjectivity of emotional responses is linked with varied knowledge about self. Positivism and negativity of emotion is very much dependent upon nature of self belief. Self belief along with self regulation help individuals to stay on the rough path of success which is essentially filled with initial hard ship and setbacks, which may come to hinder you occasionally. Self belief are affirmation by inner self which is given by your heart whenever you are getting distraction on the way or great obstacles stopping you for a while. Let us understand what the domain of self is all about.

Domain of self

We are now able to know where our mind resides inside our body. Although the mind defines our domain of self, we are always having a vague idea about self thereby knowing self becomes much difficult. Our true potential of self thus remain unexplored, which has been put in by nature enabling us to use it in fullest potential. Visualizing self should begin with seeing the physical and mental map of our body and soul. Sometimes we are amazed by the similarities of reactions shown by the people around us when they are exposed to similar situation we face. We are more amazed when we see people react differently as result of similar situation. Whatever be the difference, a person's reaction is based upon his cognitive learning of environment and emotional manifestation as a resultant of threat perception blended with decision of cognitive brain. Emotions override cognitive brain if he perceives a fight-or-flight situation. In fight-or-flight situation, people typically have a very limited range of possible responses, to enable quickening person's response time in the emergency situation. On the other hand, positive emotions explore various possibilities, present new possibilities, providing the individual with a wider range of choices and actions to opt to act on.

Positive emotions are strongly influenced by belief in self which has two components; knowing oneself and approving oneself.

Knowing yourself is nothing but knowing strength and weakness of cognitive and emotional intelligence. Finding the real capabilities within our self is much harder task than we believe. We always tend to gauge our reactions against various situations we faced earlier. If we consider them as tools for measurement, then we allow prejudice to come in and we mistakenly judge our weaknesses rather than capabilities. Knowing the capabilities does not mean discovering weaknesses but to find means to conquer weaknesses. For the sake of discovering true potential, we have to be disbeliever of Psychological determinism.

Positivism goes with enormous possibilities and optimism and refutes determinism.

Even after knowing the capabilities we cannot begin to move ahead on right path due to lack of starting power overcoming the inertia unless our self approves. The deterrent of approval are mainly negative thoughts which bind us or make us believe that we will no longer enjoy present comfort for the struggle of future fruit deemed as not to be as sweet. In most of the cases, we ignore our real strength and tolerances but focuses on obstacles and their possibilities of existence. We try to recapitulate the past instances of failure, disapproval and consequential hurt to our self. Whatever be the extent of failure, it is obvious that it has given us the learning, by emphasizing what option not to choose to avoid debacle. It is to be recalled that we are in the process of evolution and not really in the survival stage unlike our ancestors who faced in early life after creation of human race, the fear of disease, wild animal, food, shelter, cloths.

Self belief may be built up with self questioning with the help of cognitive brain. The typical questions may be like this:

What are we made for? Are we to live/eat/enjoy/spread species/let live others?

What are responsibilities entrusted to our self? Is it to protect self/progeny/all others?

What are we accountable for? Is it for our work/our idleness/ procrastination/progress?

Are we performing our task? Is it to some extent/less than desired/more than expectation?

Are we empowered? Do we require others' guidance and control, are we self sufficient or do we require guidance or are we forced to certain act or we are independent?

What are the powers within us? Are they to drive self or to succumb to odds?

Where do we store our powers? Is it in mind/soul/thought/dream/perception?

Are we driven by our thoughts? Are we driven by dream/thought and follow action of someone?

Can we control our thought? Is it under our full control/partial control/not under control?

What are forces which bind us? Is it belief/myth/superstition/health/current state of mind?

What the negative thought are for? Is it for safety/comfort/conviction/inaction?

Is it reasonable? Is it to avoid or use? Where is to be used?

Is there any limit to individual performance? Is limit defined by perception or by reality?

What we believe we can do? Is the belief based on past performance or potential?

We can go on questioning our self trying to get reasonable answers. It is not surprising that self-talk will tell you true story about you if performed seriously.

Our emotional inputs and the impacts on our brain are not only dependent on our self belief but also on our consciousness level. Human consciousness level starts to grow since 18 month of age and continually develop the awareness within us that we are ourselves. It is believed that it all starts in the reticular activating system, which is a group of diffused nerve cells in the brain stem. This sends projections to Thalamus, which in turn sends these projections through the Cortex. Consciousness is constant activation of the Cortex. To put it simply, consciousness level of individual at any point of time is the current self awareness of the individual. There are many definitions exists in psychological and theological domain. Our Bhagavat Gita says about consciousness in much detail.

Let us understand what it says.

"Avinasitu tad viddhi

yenasarvamidamtatam

vinasamavyayasya

asya it nakascitkartumarhati"

It describes the nature of soul which means it passes through the entire body and no one is able to destroy that imperishable soul. The verse clearly expresses the real nature of the soul, which is spread all over the body: it is consciousness. Everyone is conscious of the pains and pleasures of the body in part or as a whole. This spreading of consciousness is limited within one's own body.

The soul is full of knowledge of self with consciousness, which in turn means that consciousness is the symptom of soul, even if one cannot find the exact location of soul in the body, he still understands the presence of soul by the presence of his consciousness.

What we see, feel and believe and interact with outside world is dependent on our consciousness level. Our consciousness level interprets things in our brain according to state of mind or brain, which is mostly subjective.

Consciousness can be described as the quality or state of awareness of external stimuli or feelings within oneself. It has been defined as the ability to experience or to feel, the sense of self-hood. Since time immemorial, philosophers wanted to capture true nature of consciousness. However, most philosophers believe existence of underlying intuition about which consciousness is anchored.

Max Velmans, (Emeritus Professor of Psychology at Goldsmiths, University of London) and Susan Schneider (Associate Professor, Department of Philosophy, The University of Connecticut) says "Anything that we are aware of at a given moment forms part of our consciousness, making conscious experience at once the most familiar and most mysterious aspect of our lives"

Cognitive science was initially cynical about existence of various forms of consciousness, however as it progressed acquiring latest technological advancement; it has thrown light on it in limited manner.

Ned Block, Silver Professor of Philosophy, Psychology and Neural Science at New York University introduced distinction between two types of consciousness: phenomenal (P-consciousness) and access (A-consciousness).

According to him, P-consciousness means simply raw observational experience about stimuli and its nature, such as, moving or static, having any colour/sound or not etc and its reaction in receiver. These experiences, considered not to have any impact on behaviour.

A-consciousness is considered as the phenomenon where information in our brain is accessible for memorizing, visualizing, reasoning, controlling of behaviour. Therefore, whenever we visualize, perceive any information, the thought is access conscious.

Consciousness and competence

In behavioural science consciousness has been interpreted as level of knowledge about self capabilities and the interplay with its subjective competence. Scientists have identified the various level of competence in the field of training and development of any skill. Various levels of skills are associated with consciousness. Combination of competence and magnitude of consciousness level determines the area of competence. Theory of Four Stages for Learning Any New Skill was developed by Noel Burch in the 1970s at Gordon Training International. According to this theory anyone would come across the following stages of learning:

Unconscious incompetence (stage1)

Conscious incompetence (stage2)

Conscious competence (stage3)

Unconscious competence (stage4)

To elaborate let us illustrate the classic example of learning driving skill.

Stage1: Before going into learning we do not know about our incompetence. At this stage, we are unaware of the incompetence of driving skill which needs to be learnt.

Stage2: After putting some efforts, knowing the basics of driving, we come to know what shortcomings are and completely get aware of our incompetence.

Stage3. After lot of repetitions and practices, we know how to accelerate, to turn, to decelerate, to shift gears, to apply brake to stop. At this stage we are aware of competence.

Stage4: Due to repetition of same action, our skill gets enhanced over the year and reaches to that level, where we don't decide to put the brake on seeing man crossing the road suddenly or to put lower gear for slowing down. Our hand or leg spontaneously reaches to control after seeing the situation outside. It seems our brain does get involved in decision making and this stage is called unconscious competence. This level is ultimate goal for any skill set.

Processing Visual inputs inside brain

Since time immemorial, visualization had been used as a favourite tool for memorization. In fact before invention of paper, most of the knowledge passed on from generation to generation mostly through verbal communication and some contents were taught with the help of pictures, diagrams, murals, pictograms etc. Soon after paper or print media coming into existence and having been widely used, our brain had to adapt to new context of memorization which was not till then formed inherent *charac*teristic of human being. Even still now, we are more comfortable to language only to the extent of listening and speaking rather than memorizing text from print media. Still, for the profession, daily life, schooling we have to memorize the pictures, the texts, but we all

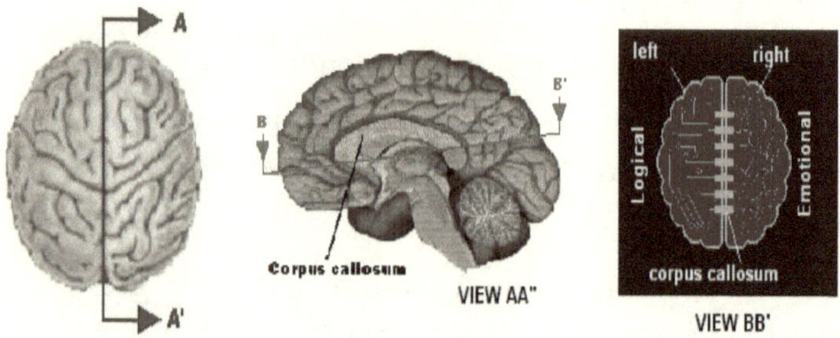

adopt picturization of ideas which is described in texts to remember easily. Our brain memorizes various things in different ways and stores information in different locations. The effective retrieval and usage of stored inputs depend on how we had stored them. Based upon location of memory storage, brains are divided into two broad regions, namely left lobe, right lobe and connecting tissues in-between (called corpus callosum); latter comes into play whenever interaction between two lobes are required. The function of human brain was little known until 60s. After several researches on brain imaging, functions of the different region of brain were to known to medical researchers. Some of split brain research involved removal of corpus callosum of brain for treatment of fits and seizure. As an outcome, surgeons had got astonishing result. Based on the various experiments, functions of the right, left lob and interconnecting tissue have been identified as below. In various hypothetical situations make left lobe, right lobe act differently, yet we can notice corpus callosum fairly optimizes the both extremes.

Left Lobe characteristics	Corpus callosum (Optimized Characteristics)	Right lobe characteristics
Logical	Selecting right input from raw data	Random, imaginative
Accuracy	Making presentable	Aesthetics
Sequential	Orchestrating resources	Random
In-depth	Finding pros & cons	Holistic
Analytical	Prevention of faults	Intuitive
Lyrics	Singing a song	tune
Looks at parts	Searching means for improvements of system	Looks at whole
Numbers or text	Remembering name of colour in text	colours
Verbal thought	Sharing idea with anybody	Visual thought
Setting goal	Putting time line with right means to achieve	Setting dream
Considers alternative	Choosing right option	Go with first idea
Organizing inputs	Assuring success	Visualizing results

Therefore we can choose best of both worlds by optimizing both side of the brain which can only be possible by stimulating corpus callosum. It is said, right brain+left brain=whole brain, which means if you stimulate both side of the brain you can stimulate connectivity of both. Stimulating both hemispheres can be performed by using both hands in various uses.

One such experiment was performed by Kazuo Satomi and colleagues (Department of Internal Medicine, Gifu University School of Medicine) in which a person keeps his eyes closed and his one hand's finger is touched by another person, at the same time he feels the touch sensation and mimic the act on opposite hand by the thumb of that hand. This test on corpus callosum is called the 'cross lateralization of fingertips test'.

Influence of self over others

We visualize and perceive people's nature and intention by their outward action and responses resulted out of interaction with others. The traits of known people become familiar with long association with them and known persons try to influence over others for their benefit. We also tend to form a first impression even if we encounter an unknown person.

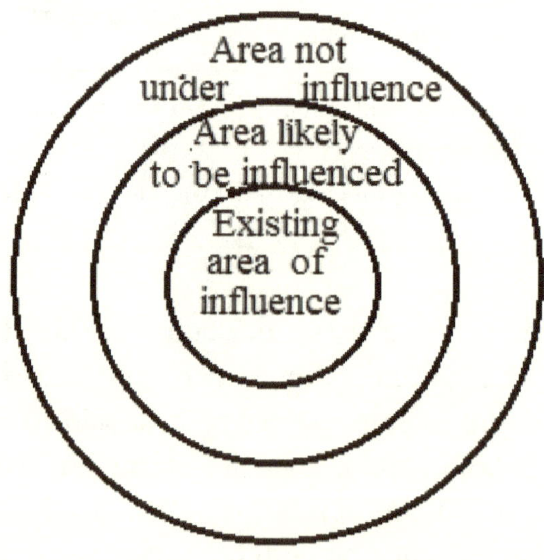

Each person is having certain area of influence, i.e. over certain people you can rely upon to cause your influence to be effective. Outside this borderline of this imaginary circle contains other persons who are unknown i.e. your influence will be ineffective on them.

(Adapted from 'The seven habits of highly effective people' be Stephen R. Covey)

We understand people's mind first by perspective and principles with respect to self. Suppose, you are approached by a person seeking help by giving him shelter for one night. You place yourself in that person and perceive that you are new to this town and somehow lost money for which you cannot stay in a hotel. You decide to ask for a shelter offered by good inhabitant of this town and seek help for some money. While considering giving shelter to stranger, you may also perceive other way. The person may be a terrorist seeking shelter for hide himself to protect from police, etc.

The nature of outcome, i.e. whether you will help him or not, will be dependent on prevailing perception at that moment and decision after getting few confirmatory responses from the persons.

Now, consider yourself in a position just as the person approaches to you. You will try to pose yourself like your first perception visualizing outcome to be positive one. Each and every query from opponent is to be resolved and confirmed to prove your stand point that you are a good person in distress.

Influencing any people for any cause, calls for strong supporting evidences which should be logical and comprehensive. Your area of influence can also be enlarged over unknown people by endorsement of known people or common person mutually and exclusively known to persons in your area of influence. The following 5E's enhance the area of influence:

Effective communication: Your influence over unknown people begins with how you touch the heart of person or group of persons you interact with. Communication is the only means to reach other person's mind. You might be aware that people first try to understand the body language and to find discrepancies with respect to what you speak. Say from your core of heart with positive conviction and your facial expression will tend to tell your story more vividly than the words you choose to speak.

Emphasize: Try to give idea of your objectives connecting broader idea of fulfilling needs of people at large. Emphasize broader aspect of how others can be benefited rather than designating objective oriented conversation highlighting the self. Benevolence and philanthropy attract everyone and liked by all.

Evidential support: Just talk of evidences, which may be used as ulterior transaction between conversations. Sales people, in general, try to persuade potential customer during tea break with evidences presented with personal touch, just like how they got benefited substantially investing in a particular fund or scheme, but they hide intention to win customer's alignment to particular fund or scheme he want to sell. Evidences of other known people can be used ingeniously presenting themselves as benefactors.

Elaboration: Elaborate the benefits with live examples and illustrations but clarify the fine prints underlying any scheme, so that people may feel they are fully informed and they are not definitely misguided.

Enamour: It acts like magnetic field by creating a magic charm over people to make them believe whatever you want to. It is the ultimate stage of power of influence, when you achieve a great recognition from large cross section of population, your words will make people spell bound, and you can then make people follow wherever you go.

Turning hostility into your favour

Influence over unknown and hostile people have been always challenging, however FBI in USA has devised a few strategic moves while negotiating hostage deal. Let's discuss Eric Barker's Blog as published in TIME's.

The characteristics of hostage negotiations underline the struggle for control that is being exercised during the negotiation process. In hostage negotiation, both the parties try to exert power on each other to influence the actions of the other.

FBI's hostage negotiation unit has developed Behavioural Change Stairway Model which indicates 5 steps to convince people to see your viewpoint to change their mind.

These are the five steps they follow:

1. *Active Listening:* Just listen to their words making then aware that they are being listened carefully and patiently.

Active listening may cover expressing brief affirmations like "yes" or simple nods. Do not try to suggest anything at this stage.

2. *Empathy:* With the help of verbal communication reach their mind where lies their emotion and the reason behind. Your role should be assisting to express the emotion not to guide anyone to make opinion or choice.

3. *Rapport:* It is the feedback of the people you negotiate after reaching their mind. With the help of empathy, rapport is built with negotiator.

4. *Influence:* At this time you have earned the trust and can influence the people by offering a solution or presenting the option to choose solution of their problem being a partner.

5. *Behavioural Change:* At this stage people the people get decisive and change their mind to be more rational, as making a choice requires logical understanding and the process evokes change of behaviour.

According to Eric, first step is the most crucial and on successful execution of the first step rest will follow well. FBI hostage negotiators have taken active listening to new height with the following techniques:

1. *Open Ended Questions:* Asking open ended question opens up mind, giving way to talk more to express, likely to lead more information about people being negotiated.

2. *Application of effective pause:* Pausing is a powerful tool, which can be used for encouraging someone to continue talking. It may also be used to control or defuse surge of emotion.

3. *Minimal Encourager:* Let them talk more without any interruptions, while giving them feedback body languages expressing that you are listening.

4. *Mirroring:* Or repeating the last few words or phrase can do the wonder. It will just give then understanding that you are not only listening but trying to understand feelings in each expression.

CHAPTER-7

Dream, Perception, Myth and Reality

"The great enemy of the truth is very often not the lie-deliberate, contrived and dishonest, but the myth, persistent, persuasive and unrealistic. Belief in myths allows the comfort of opinion without the discomfort of thought"- **John F Kenedy**

"Another mistaken notion connected with the law of large numbers is the idea that an event is more or less likely to occur because it has or has not happened recently. The idea that the odds of an event with a fixed probability increase or decrease depending on recent occurrences of the event is called the gambler's fallacy. For example, if Kerrich landed, say, 44 heads in the first 100 tosses, the coin would not develop a bias towards the tails in order to catch up! That's what is at the root of such ideas as "her luck has run out" and "He is due." That does not happen. For what it's worth, a good streak doesn't jinx you, and a bad one, unfortunately, does not mean better luck is in store." -**Leonard Mlodinow**

You might have heard about Augusto Odone, a World Bank economist, whose son Lorenzo was diagnosed with Adrenoleukodystrophy (ALD), a rare and incurable disease in his early childhood which had damaged the hearing, speech, vision and entire nervous system and he eventually turned paralyzed. The specialist doctors had said he has nothing but to watch his son dying. A man in eighties could believe the logic presented by best medical practitioners of the world as there was no treatment of disease available. He himself having high school science knowledge does not have any idea of medicine; but he ventures into studying the effects of various reagents on human nervous system and experimented with various concoction of natural reagents. Ultimately he was able to discover potent mixture of oils (Olive and rapeseed oil containing erucic and oleic acid) and did proving on his sister-in-law, which turned out to be effective and having no side effect. He pushed the mixture to his son which led to halt the ill effect of degeneration of nervous system caused by the disease. His reagent is now called 'Lorenzo's oil' and he saved his son by his own discovery. Many professionals who had claimed it was impossible, he made it possible with his limited knowledge. Hollywood had paid him tribute with a film "Lorenzo's oil" in 1992.

(Source: obituary written by Odone's son-in-law after his death in 2008)

What has motivated Odone to cultivate his high school science knowledge to search for nearly impossible? Had he dreamed of being successful in achieving his goal within his lifetime while he was already in eighties and every professional doctor has given up? What's in a dream that drives itself towards success?

So we should understand the characteristics of dream which is expressed as long standing wish yet to be fulfilled but always hoped to be fulfilled and chased for, but it is not definitely meant to be what we see during sleep.

Nevertheless, the dream itself is not sufficient to kindle the flame of desire to make it a reality. It is likely to be faded eventually, as a result of lack of motivation and positive inputs, hackneyed necessities evolving in our daily life. The sustenance of cherished dream is founded upon objectives and supported by inspiration from environment.

Dream can be qualitatively classified as distant dream and near dream, but the former dream is worth its name. If anything requires very short time to fulfil it is not worth to be called as dream, but a mere desire or necessity.

Therefore, a dream which is cherished in mind will have to keep it for long but a dream is not having potential to drive us to achieve if:

• It has not told us why we should achieve it

• It has not told us when we would fulfil it

• It has not told us how it can be achieved

"why factor" is placed in top most position, since it not only tells the objective of chasing the dream, which is obviously required for setting dream, but also enables us to alter, modify, even change the dream during the process of achievement. For chasing a dream or to nurture a dream the objective or the purpose of achievement should be fully known or else it may happen that our conscious mind would stop walking with our subconscious self with the suspicion as to why it should go in for.

The "when" factor really comes in second position as if the date becomes specific, we will find the way to achieve the required pace to fulfil. The specific date will keep pressure on us to set milestones in between. Suppose we are to go to a distant place by walk, say to New Delhi which is about 100 km away. We would set 5 milestones at a 20 KM interval, we decided to walk 20 KM a day and take rest at night in a roadside motel. By this we can reach New Delhi by walk in 5 day. We can even set fewer milestones depending upon the total time required to reach New Delhi. It is to be noted that in each case, even if the milestones are fewer it would relieve great burden of covering total distance in one go.

That is why distant dreams are better chased by breaking up into smaller milestones with specific dates.

The next comes "how" to achieve. When we could break up the entire journey into milestones and further break up into minute activity, we would better know how to achieve. As we go off for a trip, we can visualize, the traffic, our steps, our breath, the landscape around, the pothole, we would become thirsty, sip water from bottle and so on. If we notice the passage of time minutes by minute for one 5 KM, we can prepare ourselves for the entire journey.

Chasing the dream is like making a journey; we would have to prepare ourselves before the voyage; we just cannot go backward notwithstanding something important is missed by our mistake. Now we may question ourselves why aren't we always prepared to chase the big dream. Is fear to finish insurmountable tasks involved in it, or are we more adapt to undermine our true potential hidden within? Let us go back to textbook concept of perception and myth.

Perception is the understanding of brain in process of interpretation of sensory inputs in order to represent awareness of objects seen or felt from the environment. Since evolution of applied psychology in the 19th Century, understanding of perception went through various experiments by studying the brain mechanisms underlying perception. The way we see to any object, events surrounding us are the outcome of previous inputs fed into our brain and this experience can be varied from individual to individual. Significance of perception or the way of perceiving any event can be illustrated by the following example:

We are used to see the written texts in black colour over white background. Similarly solid objects are seen over two dimensional background. But when white coloured word is written over black background or letters are written in hollow, we cannot recognize instantly and properly. After inversion of colours (black into white and white into black) you will get the desired visualization.

This does happen due to preoccupied thought or perception which has been made a permanent conception in mind over a very long period of time. Whenever these conceptions are built over long time with repetition, our perception gets far off from reality.

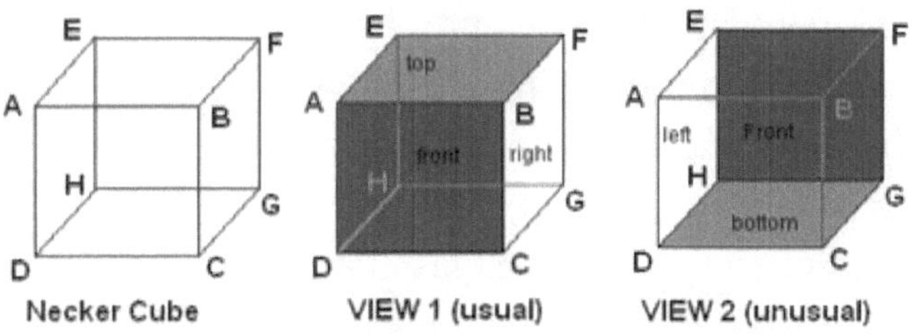

We see and feel the world around us through our perceptual systems of the brain to get a complete and stable impression, even if the sensory information is typically incomplete, inaccurate, rapidly changing and skewed by subjective beliefs. Human brains are evolved to process the inputs quickly to form an idea about the objects as seen or felt on the basis of apparent feeling.

See the picture of 1st cube (called as Necker Cube) which can be interpreted in both way "VIEW 1" and "VIEW 2".

First interpretation (view 1) of Necker cube seems possible and majority of us sees the cube with ABCD as front face, EFBA as top face and FBCG as right face as shown in View-1; all other faces are hidden to us. However, majority of us perceives second interpretation (view 2) seems to be impossible to exist. This is because,

131

human eyes are habituated to see the object from the top, and therefore its bottom surface is hidden behind its front and right face. Not only that, we have general tendency to see objects from left to right, that is why third picture (view 2) even though physically existent, apparently felt to be impossible to exist.

Based on prevailing perception over a long period of time, myths are created and believed by individual and large cross section of population. It is prevalent in animal kingdom as well. Myth is a fabulous story which is believed by individual or group of people as true that may or may not be goes well with the actual fact. On the basis of time of origination a myth may be classified as 'old', or 'new' or 'recent'. Based on relevance it also may be called as 'family myth', 'urban legend', 'perceptual or subjective myth' etc. Passing on myth may be performed by contemporary people and may also die its own death in course of time depending on occurrence. Some myths are passed on generation after generation through family fables told by ancestors to successors. However, all myths are associated with a small fact which gets distorted by repetition and deliberate exaggeration to make the story more fascinating. Perceptual Myths are subset of perception, which are subjective and play a great role deciding action of an individual. Some of the prevalent subjective myths are illustrated below.

Myth: we are lacking self potential-The elephants
Consider the case of elephants performing acts dictated by ring master in a circus. Why they are obeying orders while

they have enough strength to go as per their own will and can tear the chain they are tied with? Ever pondered why these elephants do not try to pull the chain to break themselves away? Although they have enormous power and they are put to show off it in circus act, to drag and pull much heavier objects as a daily routine, but they do not pull to tear the chain. They have been brought up since their child hood in such condition, tied one leg with a peg and during the elephants' childhood their early efforts got failed and their false belief got deep rooted that it is impossible to break the chain even if you have more strength after growing up.

We are also prone to develop such myth depending on our upbringing, perceiving inputs from our surrounding, prevailing reality frame we live within. Many times, our learned inputs, once derived with certain rules become irrelevant with passage of time and get no longer valid in present times; still we follow the same principles knowing that it is time proven.

Case study: *Myth: we certainly get hurt to attempt difficult act*

In a motivational training session of Mr. R S Tagore, where all participants (including the author) were asked to walk over a meter-long stretch of glass flakes which were made from breaking wine bottle, everyone was scared. Even if Mr. Tagore assured that no one would be harmed by doing so, no one proceeded to take on the challenge.

It was more fascinating to drag the ghost of mental blockade of performing difficult act from everybody's mind than to succeed in walking over broken glass.

We are very well aware that broken glass may cause cut, may pinch into foot leading to bleeding and bruise, even if we know it is also easier to lie on beds of thousand nails as average pressure by single nail to our skin is much less than what is required for pierce. The participants got terrified by hundreds of sharp pieces of glass beneath our foot to cross but forget the fact the more the numbers the less would be pressure to pinch.

In our day to day life, we choose to abstain from taking up challenges but to forget finding what lies beneath, or choosing the right option to succeed.

In that session, Mr. Tagore demonstrated that careful and very slow steps can alert us which glass piece we can rely upon which one to avoid giving your share of your body weight and your are done!

Eventually everyone in the hall got rid of the fear of injury and crossed the prickly path without any nicks and cuts.

It is obvious that not only we can learn from others mistake but also we can learn from others' success.

Reality: piercing is a function of average pressure on each pointed object and the impact of force

Myth: Repeated failed attempts means there is no solution-The piranhas

Experiment has been carried to a group of piranha fishes in a small glass walled tank. Foods in the tank were separated by a transparent glass wall; piranhas were kept on one side of wall and the food was on the other side. They were put into trial for several days as they were hungry and starved for food. On seeing the food over the other side of wall piranhas initially tried several times but hit on the invisible glass wall and failed. After few days the glass wall was removed. But by that time the piranhas got a bitter experience; they could not have that much courage and hope to try one more attempt. They died on starvation even if foods were accessible to them.

Case Study*: **Myth:** a few special acts are possible only by few people*

We start to believe that some special acts are possible only by few people and end up with belief that we are not among those fortunate few who can make anything and everything possible. Our perception dictates us such that even a simple thing like breaking the wooden planks by hitting with naked hand seems to be possible only by those who have mastered in martial arts.

If we see beneath, we might notice, while trying to break the wooden plank our prime motive confines to save our hands from getting hurt, which is a result of perception that anything that is harder than hand is unbreakable by hitting with hand. Our perception forces us to stop giving momentum when we just touch the surface letting not to go further but to stop it at once. It is our reflex which had been learnt through inputs from the experience while growing up. You have to make your reflexes understand what fact is and what fear is.

In a session of Neurological programming, nearly 100 participants were told to break the 1 inch thick wooden pieces by hitting hard with the naked hand. Even if the instructor told to hit hard, no pieces could be broken. It was not due to the fact that everyone was not using their best effort, but because of the momentum which fell short just after touching the top surface of the wood. When the instructor told not to hit hard but to ensure that mighty blow would reach up to bottom of the wooden piece, assuming that there is no pieces to obstruct you and that resulted in success of 80% people out of all participants.

All realized that it was the fear that retrained their hand from hitting the surface of wood. We are prone to build up such paradigm if we habitually restrain ourselves to remain in the comfort zone. In case we are not striving for shifting the paradigm, we get entangled in it and a firm false belief may set in creating a paralytic situation called paradigm paralysis.

For human being, conception or misconception can set in according to nature of individual. A person with narrow vision may not be able to expect favourable outcome after several failed attempts, but a person with lateral thinking may find easier to understand the exact cause of failure. The process of conceiving an environmental input in personalized manner based on the individual's bend of mind is called as perception. It is the conscious recognition and interpretation of sensory stimuli that serve as a basis for understanding, learning and knowing or for motivating a particular action or reaction.

Reality: Breaking of object is a function of momentum put into it, hurting is a function of resistance we receive from breaking it.

Reality

We come across the term 'reality' in day-today life in various form. You might have come across such statements 'We live in the era where nothing is believed to be taken for granted. You have to be alert in all spheres of life. Mutual trust is diminishing day by day; this is cruel and real world". Or you might have heard this statement very often "People are forgetting relationship by participating in rat race of making money. This is reality, today." Is this meant to be real reality?

Or consider this statement "Fakes are invented to imitate valuables; even if it serves the purpose, fake is fake; real is real". Can these "real" make sense really? Reality is perceived as what can be seen and felt by all in tangible form, but it can only be a relative term. Reality in future is also perceived in present time even if the event has not taken place. When the event is very likely to occur but not yet occurred till present time is also considered as real. But it can never be the absolute truth. It is just like the astrophysics which is always wrong but never in doubt. Reality can be classified in various ways.

Physical reality: Is seeing believing?

It is like we believe what we see. Whatever can be seen and felt through physical sense is believed to be true is the physical reality. Suppose, we think the sun is smaller than earth, because we see it smaller by naked eye, it will not be a physical reality. The comparison of size of the sun and the earth cannot be possible unless we place ourselves at location where earth and sun is equally distant. We can see through a powerful telescope a star burst in a distant galaxy hundreds of light year away and feel at that time we have really witnessed that event live, whereas in real sense the event had occurred few hundred years back, we have only seen its light which came to earth later. The physical reality is that the star might be turned to white giant at the time of seeing. If the object seen by our naked eye and the existence can be proven scientifically or by logic, it is physical reality.

Phenomenological reality

Phenomenology originates from the Greek word phainómenon, which means "that which appears", and lógos, means "study". According to Edmund Husserl, a philosopher and mathematician and the founder of the 20th century philosophical school of phenomenology, phenomena appear in acts of consciousness, objects of systematic reflection and analysis. He believed that phenomenology could provide a firm basis for all human knowledge, including scientific knowledge. This belief was popular up to twentieth century among the follower of Husserl. However, this philosophy loses scientific ground later on as phenomenological reality is subjective; experience of one person may not match with other, evolving some sort of spiritual reality.

Reality can also be defined as view through a window to world describing totality of all things, past and present events or phenomena, whether observable by anyone or not. It can be a world view based on individual or shared human experience with a view to describe.

Physics, philosophy, sociology, and other fields described various theories of reality. There is one popular belief that reality does not exist beyond individual perceptions or belief stating, "Perception is reality". It is reality which holds sufficiently good within the context of the matter. It is classified as Perceived reality.

Perceived reality

The law of nature suggests that everything has to undergo changes with the passage of time. There is no absolute reality. Reality is a truth within its frame of time and space. Reality is not real beyond its horizon. In a simplest example this relativistic relation of reality of different level can be described as below.

1st level: A microorganism within cellular level may be aware about the happening within the cell but cannot see the reality whatever is happening in organ.

2nd level: An organ within the body may be aware of happening inside the body but cannot tell anything about outside the body.

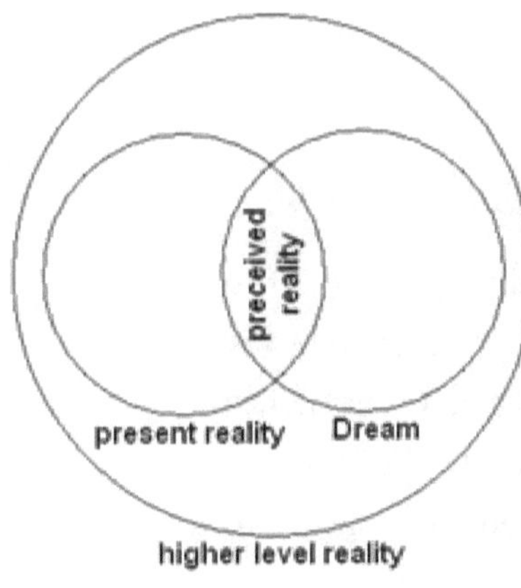

3rd level: A body may be aware of the fact of the planet but cannot tell relationship with the solar system

4th level: Planet can tell about solar system but cannot see the reality of the universe.

So on and so forth....

Indeed, reality is valid only within the reference frame in which it exists and interacts with and if we expand our horizon we may move towards greater level of reality. Living in a planet we have access to reach to cellular level. But living in earth, we see sun is moving around the earth, unless we reach to outer space (next higher level) to discover actually earth is moving around the sun. If we stay in that reality level (solar system), we cannot believe even the sun is moving.

Stepping into next level of reality level

Perceived reality is the reality within a certain framework within which that reality holds well according to perception in that frame of reality level. It is a common sub-set of present reality level and the dream (pl refer fig-5) that someone chooses to chase. Perceived reality hinders to attain dream due to negative perception exists in present reality. One cannot think beyond his or her perception, which is why perceived reality always seem to be harsher, un-attainable and not a part of dream, rather than whatever actually it may be.

Shifting frame of mind ushers the enormous possibilities

Being within a certain frame we can still step out of it with the help of available knowledge of greater reference level. Moreover if we believe that there is another level of frame the greater reality can be known. What we perceive is a limited knowledge of self and may be out of superstition.

To get rid of the perception jump into the next level and the horizon will be enormously large and earlier reference frame will definitely seem to be small and accessible.

Every achiever has stepped outside the limited framework and moved over the horizon they earlier lived in. The following steps will certainly help stepping towards the next reality level even being in a lower reality level:

"Trust everything is possible, at least, there must be close alternatives to possibility."

Today we need not to go outer space to believe earth is moving around the sun, rather from the available source of knowledge and scientific logic it can be well proven. The next reality level may be full of unfamiliar realities and uncertainties but acquiring knowledge of unknown will eventually lead you to acquire competence of the same to reach domain of next and larger reality level.

It is not only a belief but also a truth in different dimension. Perception or wrong belief has a strong base on myth and mental discomfort. Just imagine that this universe is made out of absolute singularity and each and every creature was created from the elements of nature. There is nothing seems more impossible than this colossal creation. You have the freedom to imagine rather than to think and create according to your perception. Here is the necessity of enlarging the perception to next circle of reality with the help of self belief.

Perception	Reality
I will fail to survive as I have no money	There are many people who live on nature's abundance; The concept *human needs money for decent living* is nearly 1500 years old. Even today there are people who lead life decently without earning money and also fight for others.
My next generation will fail if I have no saving	Think over how much saving has been drained by your parents to raise you. It was almost nothing in comparison to fixed assets your father accrued. You became what you are now mostly for your wish and dream.
I will be nowhere if we change the job	Over 90% of people, who changed job, have been successful. Balance has gained experienced to fight harder and become more successful in later stage.
I will be turned down if I speak out	There is no chance to be accepted if you don't speak out to reach others mind.
I will fail if I participate and everybody will laugh after me.	The winner is also a participant. There is no chance of winning without participation. If you lose, you are among those who created one winner staging the competition. Feel proud about and try the next level.

The relationship between dream and the reality is prone to be misunderstood. Reality is always linked up with hardship faced by individual, not the positive reward one may get from or dreamed about it. Popular belief runs about horrific end of every cherished dream or at least highlight the thorny way to success and achievement.

While majority of our harsh imagination when come to be true, it is much easier to tolerate, much flexible to exercise, when our visualization is perfect and the chosen way is founded upon strong base. Wherever getting result is of prime importance, end must be focused, not emphasizing the means so as to wilfully ignore the obstacles.

Dreams may seem to be a reality while we are already within a dream. When we wake up from dream, it can never be seemed as reality unless there is a dream within, i.e. if we dream about a sleep in which we are dreaming something and wake up within a dream, may be in this situation, reality may be felt within dream.

The reality therefore, is the feedback from surroundings through physical senses after waking up or being in conscious state. There is thus always a scope of doubt whether you are within your true consciousness as it is also a relative entity, can be a state of being at some point of time. Even in Indian philosophy, the reality is a myth; a form of "MAYA" which is sensed through physical organ from the physical world. It is only the super-conscious mind which can feel or see the absolute reality or truth, which is subject matter of spirituality and falls outside the realm of rational visualization.

Thus, the truth or the absolute truth pertains to philosophy and spiritual behaviour of human being.

Reality is what we can feel with our human senses, which can be achieved through humanly endeavour, can be tasted to be savoury, can be recognized within many individuals and capable of creating common understanding through individual perception and acquired knowledge which is accepted universally.

Visualization from falsified reality

Negative thoughts are well cooked in the bowl of falsified reality. Whenever an individual get distracted by the falsified reality influenced by many people or prevailing myth, his logical mind may get lost to foolish notion,

Let us go through the following hypothetical example.

Suppose you were told to stay alone in haunted house for one night without lighting up any candle or anything which can illuminate the room.

Although you have never seen any ghost or any supernatural thing in your life, neither you disbelieve its existence; you will make opinion from the gathered information about the ghostliness of the house. Before getting inside the room you could really imagine the sound of creek of the door and the cold wind blowing through the window out of your imagination.

You might envisage the sound of blowing wind, as ghostly creature entering the house. You did not have idea how it would look like, but you would imagine it won't be pleasant and friendly.

Your imagination has been obviously fuelled by the notion of prevailing supernatural objects and inputs you have got from the people and by reading fictions etc. You visualize on the basis of those ingredients even if you have no experience about visualization. Now, you could see or realize the day after passing that night, your visualization is not real or the reality is far from what you have presumed last night. Thus visualization is not necessarily being real or factual.

Optimize information by preventing information overdose

"Knowing it all before hand" has negative impact too as knowledge activates logical brain thus initiates consciousness about positive and negative aspect in decision making. Since the negative force can overpower positive aspect, knowledge of everything does not pay to make crucial decision. So shall we believe "Ignorance is bliss?" It is an irony, that after several thousand years of civilization of human race with strive to explore the unknown, we still evaluate it. In modern times also, a few of us do not visit the doctor with the scare that an incurable disease may get revealed if doctor checks up in spite of painful suffering. It is felt that hard truth will subside if it is ignored; problem will be solved automatically even if it is not addressed; whereas, most of the life problems require conscious thought to resolve and getting correct information is a must for that. However, we should avoid too much information when our capacity to handle falls short to manage information overloading. We must learn when and what to ignore. However, ignorance about ignorance is a folly one cannot afford to be with while a conscious effort about what to ignore should be well exercised. Therefore it is always blissful to optimize knowledge and minimize ignorance than falling prey to concept "ignorance is bliss."

CHAPTER-8

Making dream into reality

"A winner is a dreamer who never gives up"-**Nelson Mandela**

"Many of life's failures are men who did not realize how close they were to success when they gave up." -**Thomas Edison**

We have a popular notion about dreamer which goes like this: a dreamer can be somebody who day-dreams about things he wants to become rather than what he acts on it actually. But the contextual meaning of dreamer is somewhat different than this false belief.

The dreamers are those individuals who not only cherish big dream but to achieve the dream in time, following certain laid down principles.

The following anonymous quote may correctly illustrate the traits of a dreamer:

"A dreamer looks beyond the limits of today to the possibilities of tomorrow and sees what can be instead of settling for what is. A dreamer imagines the most wonderful new things and then finds way to make real"

The difference lies between day dreamer and dreamer is that, former one dreams about anything but never focuses on achievement and the later not only dreams big but finds ways and makes things happen to accomplish. It is obvious that dreamer has to have a big dream to cherish ignoring what he is today rather he stresses upon his capabilities to achieve extraordinary in future, thinks laterally to set principles and guide himself to achieve them conquering the hurdles coming in his way.

"Whether dreamers are born or made" is the subject of many researchers, however most of them concluded the qualities of dreamer can largely be acquired through natural upbringing and learnt from the nature or environments; however some of the traits descend from heredity. In short, it is the combination of both- what is born with and what is learnt. Let us understand some of the significant traits the dreamers are comprised of:

Be a student all through and ask "what if" to everything:

Remember being a small kid you might have asked several questions to your parents which had been answered by them and you sometimes ask back what if I do it this way or that way? In fact it is the insatiable quest to everything which can drive oneself to the bottom of everything. Recall those days of childhood, you would have followed difficult path to achieve without imparting so much effort, to learn mother tongue, bettering skill of cycling, swimming, above all you did not care pros and cons behind following certain thorny path, just believing that the road will go somewhere which is very interesting but obviously "not scaring".

Catch: Every uncertain future is always interesting and it remains interesting till you keep yourself a learner.

Be a sport, follow the heart, and ignore what your brain dictates

Have the big heart to conceive idea not limiting to your belief, your horizon of present ability. Even if any idea seems to be not viable in terms of your money you have, due to time constraint in your schedule or is not falling in core competence of your expertise etc, do not reject. Try to persuade whatever your heart tells you. It is not always brain tells you your capabilities, but your heart is always optimistic about you. The brain naturally dictates about the constraints but be selective about not listening the hurdles being broadcast, just focus on how to conquer the hurdles.

Catch: Listening to heart is important as it dictates you what you believe is important than what seem to be probable.

Never say die as nature wants tough guy to win

It is a law of nature that he survives who is the fittest. In present context achieving dream is far from getting survival techniques. But the nature poses similar challenges to overcome in way of achievement of dream. You may fall while moving, but you must get up and get along until the end is reached.

By way of chasing dream you may feel tired at the middle of journey, may get frustrated not getting result timely, may be discouraged by someone, but you must believe in yourself that you only can win the race; nobody can help you in achieving the same. If the distance is large feel that you are lone marathoner who is having only one option 'to win' if the race is completed. The attitude "never say die" will teach you the lesson of life to make you toughest fighter against all odds. Any move towards making dream real, has the obstacles in its way of achieving, but consider the obstacles are designed by nature to throw challenges to them who want to achieve it. The nature always wants the only tough guy accept the same so as to create a winner. The winner always finds the next option out of anything no matter how difficult is the solution.

Catch: If earlier attempts fail to produce result, do improve or change at least in one aspect of your action and you will certainly find the right option at the end.

Seek expertise and find the solution from other winners

While exercising various options to find most suitable one you have to keep yourself very positive. Believe there is always one more option available beyond your thought which may be the most positive than the rest. You will find at least one positive thing out of several negative ones. Searching a possibility out of seemingly impossibilities (call it challenges) you must have to accept the "yes" only. There are numerous winners who have set examples in becoming successful. Every Rag-to-rich story has the similar essence of finding solutions and choosing the right options.

Catch: *Believe there are n+1 solution to any problem on earth, if you have ability to find 1 solution, still there is "n" no of solution can be suggested by others.*

Be practical: Break the big dream into fragments

Mind matters the most, thus the dream must not seem too big to achieve, even if it actually be. It has to be broken down to smaller fragments so that mind would suggest you take smaller steps and taste the sweet smaller successes. The taste of success would led you to achieve another with full spirit and galore. See the similarities from the nature also. Evolution of species had not happened in just in years; it took millions of millions of years to create life and thereafter the monocellular organism, vertebrates, the mammals, ultimately human race. Even if we assume nature has stopped thinking producing a more intelligent species after human, the evolution of human race is still in the air. Socio-economic and psycho-somatic evolution is changing our way of living life and its perspective. It is evident that nature had been achieving the goal in steps; the success is not defined by achieving the goal only, but habituating the progress, choosing way of another success in succession.

Catch: *All big dreams are made of smaller ones, which are quite achievable with little bit of extra effort and capable of give you right impetus until ultimate goal is achieved.*

View from different perspective

Chasing the big dream will take its own course and it shall eat up small chores like chatting with friends, lot of sleep, and leisure and luxury. You will have to chase the dream, nothing else would come by. Exercise every option available; discover little known way to reach destination faster. Acquire right knowledge and skill to excel; you will be amazed to see there might be an easy solution to massive problem. Sometimes it may call for breaking the rules once in a while. It would help you see the things from different viewpoints. Think lateral, think childish, and think as if you are a bystander or an expert suggesting a stranger to do it in lot easier way than you think.

Catch: Think lateral and break the boundary of human mind.

Be vocal about your dream

Be proud to tell the progress of achievement to your peers. The encouragement from well wisher and the back bites from the jealous competitors will give you the extra momentum. You have to take every criticism into right spirit and let all inputs convert into positive output. But remember you have to short list the persons who you share the story and who are likely give you desired encouragement.

Catch: Get the emotional push to keep your logical decision rolling.

Measure the progress frequently

You must measure the progress and rate of growth. If it is slower, explore options and choose the right strategy and the path to achieve sooner. Sometimes action on right option fails to produce desired result; then think of another dimension, see whether time is ripe doing the thing bringing out fruitfulness. It is just like measuring the growth of your child; wait and have patience on outcomes until you find the difference measurable.

Catch: Change the course of action if progress falls below.

Relive child in you

You are fully aware since you have also come across your childhood and also have been associated with upbringing a child. A child is the most perfect dreamer because of the following reasons:

• They have fullest energy to chase any insipid object without knowing the pros and cons.

• They don't have the fear unless they are not frightened by someone. But grown-ups are cautious and largely scarred by negative force.

• Children are learners, always inquisitive, always tries hand on any new thing, unlike the grown-ups.

• Children likes changes and grown-ups resists change, like to stay where they are specially if it is comfortable.

• They do not mind criticism, back bites they do and keep on doing what their heart tell them to do, grown-ups decides what their brain guides them to do.

It is the child who can think from the heart which guides to achieve greatest feat by following an optimistic path; on the contrary an adult mind thinks by the brain, it will tell you to be cautious, safe with present condition, will tell you pessimistic view of uncertain future..

Develop capability for going back to basic

In today's' world you may think you won't live without cell phone, electricity, television, air conditioners and many other technological gadgets which made our lives comfortable. But we should and must be prepared for any eventualities where we can live without any of these. Feeling of comfort is mental perception, you can try to develop minimalist attitude towards using them. It will enable you to take any venture where risk is involved. You can practice it by camping in a jungle, night out in a lonely place where such amenities are not available.

Relive the possibility thinker within you

Let us go through the old story of mountaineer who had lost ways in snow storm over a mountain cliff and suddenly he found himself hanging from a branch of broken branch of a tree. He almost had lost his consciousness, after gathering all his remaining strength, he screamed "Is there anybody to help him out?" He heard a voice beneath the deep trench "Yes dear I am there to help you, if you believe in me, drop yourself down, I will catch you safely." He again screamed "Is there anybody else" There was no answer. He screamed again "I believe in you, are you there?" "Yes I am waiting".

He dropped himself finding no other solution to escape.

There are rarest of rare occasion when you would find only one solution to go ahead depending upon your gut feeling. In fact, majority of cases there are multiple ways out which have great possibilities to happen and we choose out of our gut feeling. For deciding day-today life decision we go with our gut feeling for choosing from many possibilities. However, whenever we are in a fix to decide any better option to go in for a crucial solution, we just do not think of possibilities, but we let the thought of impossibilities. In many such options it is better to find out optimized solution maximizing the yield and reversibility, which may not be the best, but it would fetch you satisfaction and if result is not obtained as per satisfaction it can be reversed.

Develop Simulator within you

As you are already aware, certain future events are envisaged through learned ingredients of past events through the process of simulation. Although creativity has nothing to do with adoption of learned inputs for preparation of simulated events, however, visualization and creative skill are essentially required for imagination of each detail prior to its actual occurrence and skill for analyzing consequential effect therein. In order to enhance analytical skill required for key inputs of past events, critical thinking process with probabilistic approach shall be fostered within yourself.

Suppose you have experience of raising fund for your college's annual fest and you are required to utilize the same for raising fund for lone and elderly people at some old age home. You go back to your college days and try to analyze what the activities you performed for choosing potential sponsors, how they were persuaded, what were excuses you received from reluctant individuals, how the fund was optimally utilized. Your probabilistic approach would identify the potential donors, means of persuasion and other processes would be perfected through your critical thinking process, creativity and heuristic approach (in few places). Creativity is one of the most important traits to be a simulator as it is frequently required to collate the inputs to make future event presentable and realistic.

The car and the head light effect

The entire journey to destination from where you are now is too long; sometimes it's very difficult to visualize the total journey; still we can start the voyage without knowing the entire road map. Imagine you are travelling at night in a car with headlights on. With the headlight you can see only a few furlongs ahead but you have to take the helm for entire journey of hundreds of kilometres. But you obviously know that after completing that small stretch, you will see the next almost similar to what you have already come across. Anything new happened to pass can be seen vividly with the headlights within its maximum capacity. The process repeats until you reach the destination. This gives a fair idea about simulation of new inputs to fabricate newer objects to visualize. Constantly you are getting updated with new insights.

Therefore, observations come into action to choose the important input for usage for building up insight and experience. The technique of simulation gives the multiplication effect to this process. Being a simulator nurturing the following skills will evolve simulator within you:

Lateral thinking

It is important to think out of box to get the best outcome. Possibilities are unlimited if you think beyond the boundary. It is believed that a child can better adopt lateral thinking and with the growth of the child the natural power of lateral thinking tends to get diminished. In a bid to keep lateral thinking afresh you have to keep the child in you alive forever. Lateral thinking is nothing but a painting with creative imagination having all colours, composition and perspective. True lateral thinking can be exercised if you are totally free of prejudice, superstition, false-belief, fear of failing etc. The complete freedom from anything will result in culmination of great and limitless ideas.

Picturizing imagination

You always tend to paint pictures with familiar objects based on easily visualized imagination. This is the way mind usually draws picture, But it is also true if any image is difficult to conceive is also difficult to paint. Let us understand how an artist paints which will help you understand the proper way to conceive a portrait of your future.

1. *Believe in yourself:* Even if the reality is harsh and difficult to achieve goal, your inner self may think differently. The opinions of majority are not always true or cannot be followed. Believe in yourself and you will find the picture getting clearer.

2. *Believe in natural happening:* Putting each and every detail for composition of picture is better done in stages. Whatever you conceive better paint it, which is not conceivable or you cannot see the firm outline, keep it aside. Leave it to nature, it will give you cue how to brighten the figure. See the half-done picture after some time you will finish it better.

3. *Test against the time:* The perfect picture can be drawn in repeated steps. However, every time you modify picture should be better and sharper than the previous edition. If judgment is assisted by better wisdom gained with passage of time it becomes time proven and let it be like that.

4. *Extend the observation tool:* Whenever we find difficulty in observation through naked eye, we must resort to microscope, satellite picture, and telescope etc. if more details are demanded. To be able to search the right thing you have to find through public resources like book, web, even meeting friends, teachers, experts would be fruitful. Your have also to believe that somewhere some time the answer lies and you are able to find the same.

A dream may lie in dormant state unless you work on it shape into a reality. A lot of hard work blended with good qualities can evoke the pursuit to achieve the dream. Ponder upon nurturing these qualities which will surely help you grooming as a dreamer.

1.*Commitment:* It is believed that Mahatma Gandhi would have failed to draw the crowd in national freedom movement unless dedication is seen by the people to influence them to fight for the country. The bigger the dream the more dedication is required to achieve it. It is not only to be put to work but also to be felt by anyone surrounding you. Gandhiji has shown to people of India that being committed to a great mission paved other good qualities to reinforce the great cause and to win over all odds. Commitment to self needs listening to heart which is a private decision to act upon. Since committing privately has no binding on society or public at large, you are not bound to follow. In general, commitment in public compels social individual to follow through on it, to avoid social rejection or to get rid of cognitive discord.

2.*Vision:* You must see beyond the horizon to foresee what and when a great is to happen, when and how the hurdles will diminish with the passage of time. He or she has to take certain key step towards achieving the certain mission. It is essential to foresee what is going to happen in far future.

3.*Transparency and magnanimity:* It means giving credit where it is due. Think of a magnanimous leader who ensures that credit for successes always goes to right persons and to spread throughout followers. It is also true that the true leader takes personal responsibility for failures which is called reverse magnanimity. It helps creating confidence about themselves and their leader to perform independently and team works better and get closer. If you are achieving your goal through teamwork, it is very important to mind individual goal of each member and help achieving them, your goal will be achieved automatically.

4.*Consistency:* Being consistent not only help to maintain the momentum towards effort put in action but also can create a habit which transforms into positive behaviour. While our aim is to achieve our goal, our process embodies visualization in each step. Consistency is achieved by regular feedback of actions you put into for moving ahead towards desired goal and correction or alternation of any action proved to be fruitless and counter-productive

Making dream into reality requires setting goals as we know there is thin line exists between dream and goal and these two are separated by time line. Thus, if you wish your dream work for you, convert it into goal, set time line for each steps of dream.

If you say I would become a billionaire, it's a dream whereas if you say I would become billionaire by 31st Dec 2020, it would be goal or target. Just writing the ultimate goal does not work for you. Let it be translated by smaller achievable parts, suppose you write creating wealth of 1 million by next year end, creating 10 million by next two years and so on.

It is always better to put your goal in writing along with the target date and the date of achievement. Any delay in achievement would eventually strike you to find out means and failure would let you explore alternatives; choose the right option to go ahead.

To have your entire dream fulfilled you have to follow certain steps. Dreamers are none other than leaders who plan every step in advance who visualize all unpredictable events so as to minimize the surprises in life. The leadership qualities in a dreamer are not often congenital, but it can be developed systematically.

Stepping stones of getting your dream fulfilled may be like this:

Set the dream

Setting the dream is the most difficult action in the process. The dream must be significantly large requiring substantial efforts to put in to give success a status worth of it. However, setting goal is nothing but a plan without resource and timeline. Therefore crystallized idea about of your wish, resources and time required for it can guide you to create dream out of cherished desire prevailed within you for long time. Goal may be driven by desire only, not necessarily be derived with the logic.

Frame the picture (Plan with resources)

Framing the picture is just like finishing every detail on the painting, with colour, form, composition with characters, objects, location. Framing signifies end of reversible process of editing or touch up on the painting and placing it permanently in specific location of brain where you can easily see and enjoy whenever you like see; each time you see the picture you will get identical view.

Visualize where you desire to move

Suppose your dream is to own a Ferrari. Define the color of exterior, define the interior color, décor and features etc. feel the ambience, feel the whoosh while passing through a tunnel, feel your companion beside you and her jaw dropping wow and feel the destination. You may get fantasized about any of your frenzied desire but never indulge on it for long as it may eat up energy required for your action.

Set the goal (Activity and target date) (Plan with resources and target date)

Dreams transform to goal when time line is added to each activity. Target date shall be chosen in such a manner that it would not be too difficult to achieve and obviously does not result in losing motivation in fighting all odds coming in your way. It must be realistic but shall have definite amount of challenge to lure you taking the good taste of it. While planning with resources optimized optimistic approach will be most fruitful way to progress, rather than following a pure optimistic path.

Visualize Milestones in the road map to accomplishment

Every distant object cannot be achieved in one day. Even, you have to wait for years to happen what you desire. The year is obvious to end at the yearend but at the same time it can be breakable by months, days, hours, minutes and seconds to make you feel easier when you are closer by one second, two second and keeps your clock ticking. Each big dream has obvious smaller parts which may take shorter time. Identify those milestones to ease your painful waiting.

Arrange the milestone and the means to achieve (Plan with resources)

You need to arrange the milestones in chronological order. Having arranged in proper sequence you are to identify the means to achieve and the alternative plan in case it is impractical. Means to achievement is nothing but effective resource management. You should think of when and how much money is required to be invested, you also got to know where manpower, influence and other resources are needed.

Visualize the means

Means to an end is not less important than end itself. Smaller milestones requires little effort to reach, but requires visualization to identify. Every known resource tends to change with respect to elapse of time. The projected milestones require anticipated and time proven resources to rely upon. Plan for alternative resource assigned to specific milestone.

Analyze (Get feedback with secondary source)

Before going ahead with the plan, analyze with respect to data from secondary sources like experts, friends, well wishers even rivals to have your plan tested for confirmation. In case any important cue is obtained, change the course of action.

Visualize cue from the heart

Listen to your inner pulse. Let the heart supersede brain making decision to kick start and make the voyage.

Go back to goal if your intuition says no

It is very important to satisfy self to accept difficult goal. In case your goal does not get the nod from your heart, analyze goal, alter, modify even change it for the sake of your heart. Sometimes set goals initially were perfect for that time but do not hold well with the passage of time, you are required to find out a time proven goal and start over again.

Visualize the effect of time on set goal

What logic cannot understand the effect of time on goal may be ascertained by the visualization. Simulate by projecting present scenario to future, take the mental snap of the goal. In case you find chosen goal is matching to the mental snap you do not have to worry, just go ahead for implementation.

Go ahead to implement (Act)

On setting a frozen goal just implement the action plan with resource. It is the real beginning of achievement, truly being said, beginning is half done. Get the balls rolling after a good start to take the taste of achieving first milestone.

If does not work fine analyze hurdle and explore means to overcome (Plan)

Visualize the hurdle keeping focus on means to overcome

The hurdle embodies negative energy, thus identification of the same requires rationality. Thus visualization of means to overcome hurdles shall be the objective which must be kept at the back of mind, so as to stay motivated in finding means and not losing momentum in finding the hurdles.

Still if it does not work for you explore different options (Get the feedback))

Visualize various options to and choose the right one to go ahead

Choosing the right one must be certified by your heart; give the green signal to cognitive brain to execute the plan.

Choose the right option and go ahead (Act)

You are now at work. Put your all effort work for you. Invest resources keeping the focus on time allocation so that it is executed on time. Track time on specific frequency to alter course of action if efforts are not working effectively.

Achieve Milestone

You achieve the milestone. Celebrate first success. Verbalize and get the positive energy from peers and well wishers.

Achieve next and so on by displacing the obstacles keeping the ultimate goal in mind. Just go on getting the taste of achieving the first get going to achieve next.

Set the next dream

Achievement is not static; rather it is like endless journey and it calls for setting stage for another dream to make it reality. Repeat first step.

Case Study: Foil wrapper to wrapper tycoon: the success story of a dreamer (Source Forbes India Article Changing Lane –The Wrapper tycoon)

The spark of entrepreneurship in the 16-year-old Sudip Dutta have gone unnoticed till he stepped into India's financial capital Mumbai, following a family setback from successive deaths of his father and elder brother. His father served as security personnel in Hindustan Fertilizer Ltd and lived in modest accommodation in Bidhannagar colony of Durgapur city. As he became sole bread earner for his family, he had just traded off his dream of higher education with economic opportunity in Mumbai.

He had got his first opportunity in Mumbai in a small pouching unit where he worked as a packer, loader and a delivery boy. The small unit was making loss; however, he did not forget to learn from opportunity to learn the foil business inside out. Around 1991, when the owners decided to sell out the unit, he moved in with his unique offer. He paid his entire savings Rs. 16,000 and with the promise that any profit for the first two years would go to the original owners. He became the owner of the company Ess Dee Aluminium.

His second acquisition was India Foils from Vedanta for Rs. 130 crore which took place after 17 years which was the first company to roll foils in Asia, way back in 1936 but making loss for long. Vedanta Group, which has a much bigger turnover than Ess Dee, earlier bought it from the Khaitan group and tried to turn it around but failed even after lot of effort initiated by turnaround specialist and founder of Vedanata, Anil Agarwal.

As he had been eyeing for expansion, he kept a close watch on India Foils for several years and knew its problems and remedial measures. He understood whatever Vedanta had tried to change the profile of company has resulted to complications. His objective was to become the biggest foil maker in the country and thus acquires India Foil.

On acquisition, Dutta relisted the company on Bombay Stock Exchange and later on reopened one of the three units in Kolkata and started selling its products. Earlier this year, the foil maker's profit and loss account, turned positive at the EBITDA (earnings before interest, tax, depreciation and amortization) level.

Today, he sits on the top floor of Ess Dee House, the corporate office of the Rs. 500 crore businesses he has built over two decades who once worked on a daily wage for Rs. 15.

What made him successful?

Like every rag-to-rich success stories, phenomenal rise of Sudip Datta, resulted from his right attitude of winner, acquisition and honing skills wherever he lacked and utilization in right time. Let us explain the key attributes towards his success:

•He moved to Mumbai to search for an better opportunity, denying a job search in locality or to start a low key job like rickshaw puller or auto driver. He created a greater possibility to find the right opportunity to opt.

•The most important turning point was the first acquisition of Ess Dee Aluminium. It has greatest significance as he thought of something which could seem impossible to anyone. He proposed to owner with such a buying price that no one can believe, the owner would agree with. Secondly, he thought of out of box, instead of searching for another job, he boasted to own the unit with a small saving.

He let his dream verbalized without thinking whether it is impossible and impractical or not, just materialized his out of box ideas.

•He knew inside out of the prey-the first acquisition as he was working as employee. The approach to workmen had been developed at this stage to handle the issues, related to grievance and desire of the employees. He acquired knowledge about the profit and loss of company, knew the secret of taking the loss making unit to profit making much before he bought the unit.

Right knowledge and in depth understanding gave him cutting edge to overcome hurdles.

•As he nurtured the company, he kept on watching the rival India Foil and acquired the requisite information and cause behind the loss of the unit.

His foresight and optimism keep him rolling.

•He made the second acquisition of India Foil at right time. He acquired the unit at opportune moment, when earlier owner turned pessimistic about the turnover of company. He got a very good negotiation for buying price.

Patience, foresightedness, presence of mind gave him competence to choose right time and he acted on it without delay.

•He had set up another foil rolling mill in Daman and generated revenue over Rs. 100 crores.

He never ignored bottom line, considered step by step building wealth.

•He had curved a niche for himself among pharmaceuticals companies like Pfizer, Glaxo Smithline and Novartis, which generated continuous generation of revenue and building assets.

He built brand image and recognition for himself to influence people.

•He created options, when he was recognized as potential competitor, Indal, stopped supplying him with the basic raw material (as the A.V. Birla Company itself was in the packaging business), he quickly opted sourcing the material from an overseas company.

He created options and chose the right one without delay.

Is success an optimized output of determinism, freewill and randomness of events?

Let us analyze the above case study in light of determinism, free will and randomness. If we see the crucial factors affecting the ultimate outcome, the most important event seems to be untimely death of "Sudip Dutta's father and elder brother. Hadn't these events been happened, Sudip Dutta would definitely not have moved to Mumbai and successive events won't be a reality. Therefore behavioural and socio-economic determinism came into play as death of his father ceased the family earning and this cause effected to throw him into survival struggle.

But Sudip Dutta had to take a call whether to move out or to stay back trying opportunities in Durgapur. He could have stayed back to his native place doing something else as others are doing well. He rather had chosen to do something big or just enhance the possibilities of opportunities by going to Mumbai and thus his free will and probabilism had also played its crucial role defining his future.

The series of opportunities came across are random events which had been made as possibilities and actions which he implemented were part of his free will as may be seen from the facts.

Behind almost all success stories there are three ingredients well blended by nature.

CHAPTER-9

Combating negative logic and emotions

"If you really want to do something, you'll find a way; if you don't, you'll find an excuse."

- Frank Banks

"Obstacles don't have to stop you. If you run into a wall, don't turn around and give up. Figure out how to climb it, go through it, or work around it." **- Michael Jordan**

I recollect a brawl of classmates happened in my student days while two rival groups in our college campus; they were fighting tooth and nail over a trivial issue. One group was trying to get hold of the other with improvised weapon while the other group, which was smaller in size, had to flee away from scene to defuse the situation. One fellow of smaller group hid himself behind a nearby bush. Incidentally he was found by one of his opponent group. Then everyone cornered him for a final assault. He came out saying "come on hit me and beat me to death".

All students in that group got baffled, being not able to decide action on him who has just now surrendered. Finally, all agreed to let him go without any scratch.

The incident renders two things

1.*The group dynamics of the mob:* They picked up iron rods for a tiny issue which can never be thought to fight for by an individual. Even a trivial issue may get emphasized and fuelled by wrong perception and can hurt the group's self esteem which turned into raising the alarm to fight.

2.*Individual conscience:* When the victim surrendered, individual conscience prevailed which overwhelmed the group's decision. When he screamed "beat me to death", the group's ego got raised again feeling that he is at the mercy of the group. The individuals in that group recovered the lost esteem and forgave the opponent.

If we look deep into the scenario and understand the psychology of the person described above, we'll see he was fighting against negative emotions with negative logic which produced positive result! What is negative logic exactly? Let us understand with more clarity.

Negative logics are fallacies and excuses to relieve pseudo-rational mind from responsibilities, to shy away from hard work, to create a comfort zone around or may be to resist changing the current state fearing losing present comfort. Pseudo-rational mind always tries to find negative logic in everything requiring efforts, and even if minute efforts are involved tries to explore great short term benefit. Such state of inactivity is driven by negative emotions or by passive emotions.

Shlomo Hareli, a social scientist at university of Haifa (Israel), stated in his paper in ISRE conference in 1996 that we tend to make excuses or justification when demand for explanation of questionable action causes uneasiness or dissatisfaction. According to him our reaction will be of primarily three types- avoidance, admission or defence.

On agreeing upon the above hypothesis, there may be instances for various situations where we make excuses or justifications.

Avoidance: When we tend to save ourselves trying not to face the explanation, assuming the fact that it will not create any further damage and will fade out with passage of time.

Admission: Wherever we cannot find any reason to defend, we admit our fault and make appeal for forgiving the mistake.

Defence: In situation admitting the mistake can potentially harm our image, that why we give reasoning or justification why we did it or pass it on to others protecting ourselves.

Negative logic is just like excuse which always hides the truth and always demands for explanation even if it is not required. In most of the cases it gives negative excuses to us for easy escape; however, it cannot mitigate the damage in long run. The best tool to fight against self defying negative logic is to employ positive emotions.

Negative and passive emotions may appear as game spoilers as they hinder the path of progress very often. Passive emotions are the passage of positive fantasies evolving out of positive emotions which extract so much emotional energy that left over energy falls short to overcome inertia to change. These passive emotions such as calm, balanced, cautious, composed, comfortable, contented, defended, experienced, fulfilled, gentle, grounded, guarded, happy, humble, protected, peaceful, relaxed, relieved, simple, secured, settled, satisfied, stable, tender, tolerant etc. are having potential of sapping energy if not cautiously and timely utilized.

The following illustration of passive emotions will help understand how negative logic is created to protect passive mind:

Passive emotions	Negative thought background	Negative logic	Negative Effect
Calm	Do not react	Reaction will invite argument and will attract additional effort, unlikely to produce result	Letting the things happen
Balanced	Please everyone, no one is to be hurt	Present comfort zone will be disturbed	Patronizing the evil
cautious	Be on safer side rather than taking venture	Venture is likely to produce risk and hazard	Lack of implementation of great idea
Comfort-able	Everyone should work but to achieve comfort	Everybody works ultimately to gain comfort	Lack of hard work to progress further
Relaxed	Take it easy	Thriving for anything requires hard work and mental tension	Lack of extra effort
Settled	Everyone should work to settle somewhere even if goal is unaccomplished	Thriving hard for difficult goal disturbs normal life	Lack of drive

While most of excuses are focused to avoid the physical discomfort and abuse, which primarily eyes on short term disadvantages ignoring the long term benefits. Here are some of the top excuses being faced by us:

I am very busy or I don't have time

In fact, most of the situations in certain phases of life, we do not have long stretches of time but we do have several time gaps lying between our smaller activities in day to day life. We do indulge passive lifestyle like watching television in long stretches consuming the most available longer stretches in daily routine.

How to prevent: For strenuous activity like physical exercise, we avoid doing it as not having longer time spaces. In fact, the activity if broken into several pieces like two shorter duration in morning, two shorter durations in evening, it can be fitted well into our schedule. We may club other must-do activities of shorter time into one long time slot to create long time gap available for stressful activities.

I am physically exhausted

In order to avoid work out or any other stressful work, we resort to this excuse, but fact is different than we believe. We are guided by our perception that we are physically exhausted, whereas in most of cases we are mentally exhausted.

How to prevent: Just think that physical work outs can actually energize you to cope with more physical strain as exercise produce endorphins which give you energy to do more.

Men cannot understand complexity of woman's brain

In reality, men do not try to read the mind of women as men are a bit selfish about their serving their own interest. If it is understood, men do not deny their wish and even find difficulty in searching counter logic to defy. Thus men stay and enjoy the state of blissful ignorance.

How to prevent: Show magnanimity to others, gives due credit to whatever womenfolk contributes in a family and society at large.

I won't try as everybody has tried but failed

Failure to achieve something inherently has certain individual reasons and few external factors responsible for it. It is broadly understood that external factors are only responsible for the resulting failure, whereas individual lacking is the most important factor in this process. We try to avoid hard work by believing the logic which satisfies logic and help retain our comfort zone.

How to prevent: Analyze cause of failure in proper perspective. Focus only on success stories of winners and build up positive attitudes.

If you control diet, you may invite malnutrition

As we grow older and progress on the path of economic freedom, we tend to indulge in all pleasures and eventually form the habit of overeating. Day to day requirement of nutrition falls as physical activities and metabolism tend to get reduced. In most of the cases, eating less is just for our health, whereas we feel other way round, as less eating will result in malnutrition.

How to prevent: Eat less of high calorie food; choose stuff with more in roughage. Eat more frequent but less in quantity, drink water more.

We do not put our effort if we commit 'will try our level best'

Most of us perceive word 'trying' means an effort yielding less result or no result. Even if 'level best' is added, the listener understands the statement with less or no commitment. Sometimes the passage gives the teller relief as nothing is committed. In such cases assurance made to anybody gets falsified eventually as self commitment is not involved.

How to prevent: Find the statement where you can get yourself committed to achieve such as "my furthest level is up to this or that, I will give up beyond that".

I don't start exercise as I don't want to be fall out

Statement is much alike 'I won't try as everybody has tried but failed'. Having been negatively charged, one can easily find excuse to refrain from work out rather than finding the way out to continue with the habit.

How to prevent: It is better to form habit first with less exercise, as rigorous exercise can devour your effort to continue in long run. On staying in less exercise regime for at least two month or so, add on more.

It's our hard luck that caused failure/ Real world are filled with uncertainty, just leave everything on destiny.

Luck is made as scapegoat when failure sets in due to lack of individual effort and to protect self image. Everybody gets rid of undermining self, thus choose to popular options. Moreover, leaving matters to destiny relieves self from putting blame.

How to prevent: Analyze the possibilities with respect to real scenario. Put the logic and let principle of indifference in physical world come in.

Why to achieve success, when we are enjoying our present

The taste of elusive success is different from enjoying comfort as underachiever. Even if we try to appease ourselves by not being after our great goal as hard toil is required to put into it. The statement is a defence mechanism to deceive others and to satisfy self as well.

How to prevent: Analyze your situation whether you are satisfied within yourself. In case your inner self clear yourself then go for achieving further.

Positive Emotions

The emotions, such as joy, exhilaration, high spirit, inquisitiveness, exploratory thoughts etc. are pole opposite to negative emotions. Unlike the negative emotions, positive emotions are meant for flourishing, expanding horizon of thoughts and looking bright side of things, and are certainly not meant for quick survival. It is identified by its inherent characteristics of 'giving energy' which not only boosts up self but also has potential to amplify the magnitude to influence people at large. The positive emotions do not have any immediate survival value, because they take one's mind off immediate needs. American behavioural scientist Barbara Fredrickson, has conducted randomized controlled lab studies on various participants in which they are randomly assigned to watch films that induce positive emotions like amusement and contentment, negative emotions such as fear and sadness. When compared to people in the other conditions, participants with positive emotions show heightened levels of creativity and innovativeness. Positive emotions play a role in the development of long-term resource such as psychological resilience and flourishing. Positive emotions carry a sign of flourishing, thriving and expanding life fulfilment rather than simply surviving life, they can also help create affluence in the present and in the future, as it positively broadens and builds one's set of thought-action equation, leading to increased resources and more satisfied lives.

Managing emotions with logic

Efforts are on since long time back to manage negative emotion like invasive wrath, profound hatred, agonizing grief and morbid fear. The weapons to control over uncontrollable emotions were the subject of research for psychologist in every part of globe in different era.

Scientific knowledge of being irrational or rational is still undergoing change. Even after learning the reasoning and rationality our intuition, beliefs, superstitions prevail over rational thinking.

Even today, popular belief runs like this: when we want to go to south, bus goes to north. Suppose we are expecting something favourable and it happens to be reverse of what we desire. But sometimes whenever things turn out in our favour, we forget to appreciate our good effort. Our belief is that expectation meets achievement only when our luck favours. It seems foreseeing future is entirely dependent on belief, luck and even on superstition. We never try to give due credit to our effort; even we do not believe there is any logic behind happening any event we forecast in the past. Putting a mathematical approach to our belief and expectation seems to be more farfetched. Introduction of perplexing and complex mathematical expression to our emotions is not quite new; the legacy came from the time of Thomas Bayes, the noted English mathematician of eighteenth century. However, mathematical interpretation of human emotions and logical control of the same certainly put individuals on the path of rationalism. Let us first understand minute difference between common terms which we use every day and close analogy to terms used in mathematical domain.

Possibility: By this term we generally understand Probability (favourable outcome/total outcome), however in mathematical terms it means every outcome that can be possible to occur.

Luck: Good luck or luck means theological determinism by which favourable events happen beyond our expectation. In mathematical terms, there is no such determinism exists; instead expectancy is quantified even if it is least possible to happen and which are random in nature.

Success: It generally means attainment of big dream. In mathematics, it is probability of happening of any events within certain time frame.

Learning: Generally means acquiring knowledge. In mathematical terms it is incremental confirmation (Resultant probability after each subsequent evidence taken into account as learning)

Intuition: It means gut feelings or sixth sense by which we choose options without any reasoning. In mathematical terms it is predictive power (conditional probability/unconditional probability)

We have seen our mind is comprising of positive and negative emotions, the former drives us to overcome hurdles in path of success and later hinders us by blocking the positive emotion to react in right way. Most often we discover that it is not the real obstacle which tries to block our way but our negative emotion which blocks our vision to see beyond the apparent obstacles.

Positive emotions such as joy, brilliance, respect don't seem as useful as negative emotions like fear, disgust, anger for instant reaction to cognitive input as positive emotions does not produce specific action for survival as those sparked by negative emotions. However, our ancestors have the positive emotions in place to grow and expand their successor, giving positive environment like love, care, compassion.

According to Dr. Barbara Fredrickson positive emotions, like joy, interest, contentment and love broaden an individual's momentary thought–action repertoire just like joy sparks the urge to play, interest sparks the urge to explore, contentment sparks the urge to savour and integrate, and love sparks the urges of recurring cycle of each of these within safe, close relationships.

Broadened mindsets broaden people's momentary thought–action repertoire in such way that positive emotions promotes discovery, creative actions and ideas & social bonds, that build that individual's personal resources which in turn act as reserves that can be drawn on in future for coping up eventualities, survival, achieving good health &well being.

Let us discuss the reason behind creation and existence of these two great opposing mind forces.

Negative emotions

Negative emotions are part of our emotional driving force existed from creation of mankind which are essential as survival kit, but it is able to edge out positive emotions at any moment. Professor Jeffrey Cohn, university of Pittsburgh, says, negative emotions are to flag a problem and tell you to fix it. But positive emotions appear to win over time because they let you build on what you have.

"We found that as positive emotions go up, there comes a point where negative emotions no longer have a significant negative impact on building resources or changing life satisfaction," Cohn says. "Positive emotions won't protect you from feeling bad about things, nor should they. But over time, they can protect you from the consequences of negative emotions."

Negative emotions are stronger than positive emotions as nature designed it to react fast for survival, and for that reason it has to surge within the pool of emotion to suppress everything else. If we suddenly see a tiger very close to us we get frightened and cognitive brain cannot analyze the situation to give you the right action to do in time, but emotional brain will let you know signalling the lower limb for fleeing away. Fear is stronger as it emerges than the courage as required for you to save your soul on time. However, the negative emotions like fear, anger, hatred, sadness, procrastination creates a wrong perception in mental frame leading to creation of myth which is more dangerous than untruth. Myth is a lie in disguise which behaves as unrealistic truth.

Managing Negative Emotions: Fear and myth

Amongst all of negative emotions, fear has the greatest potential of being obstacles in your way. It can let you down thinking of emerging danger or discomfort which most of cases are non-existent. Fear of many kinds may be associated with anyone that gets deep rooted with the inputs from the circumstances and frequencies of occurrence. Some of the fear one may encounter are like these:

Face of fear	What lies beneath	Fact contrary to myth
Resistance to change	Fear of uncertainty, lack of information	Changes can bring about exposure and multi-skill, get stronger to fight odds.
Lack of team work	Fear of unknown people/situation	Team work reduces stresses of mounting pressure of big goal and people tend to get motivated to share achievement.
Anger	Fear of losing self esteem	Anger does not protect self esteem. Rather defending by logic has stronger effect.
Lack of hard work	Fear of discomfort	Hard work satisfies self, resulting in mental comfort. In no case, we do not need to shift mountain, causing physical discomfort.
Procrastination	Fear of discomfort, fear of failure	Procrastination does help reduce load, but accumulates more load for near future.
Lack of initiation	Fear of lack of skill	Skill is upgradable and available everywhere.
Fear to say "NO"	Fear to hurt others, losing self image	Speaking truth is liked by majority of people.
Fear to negotiate	Fear to lose ego	Whatever people speak in response is not from the heart. Negotiation reveals the truth.

Most of the fears are subsets of fear of uncertainty and fear of discomfort. These fears are grown up with building up myths, half truths, taboos which are more dangerous than the falsehood. The myths are very much friendly with negative emotions.

Negative emotions can be managed tactfully with the positive logic. Consider these positive statements:

Negative emotions	Positive statements (logic)
I fear being a millionaire because it requires hard work and there is little time available.	If I work hard I will gain respect and recognition and I can manage time
I will fell ill if I work hard	Hard work will never impact on my health, in fact I will gain good health by putting physical work.
I fear being a achiever because it attracts bad people and I will lose money	I will gain skill of judgment and be capable of protecting money
I cannot have time to enjoy mid-day sleep	I can avoid mid-day sleep because it is harmful to health, who cares mid-day sleep?
I fear being a winner in sprint event because it needs prolong practice	Prolong practice will make me stronger and I can succeed to win
I fear to lose in the event because only one wins out of many people	I may be the winner, if I get myself stronger than anyone and a good fight is not less than win
I fear to change because it is uncertain	Even if uncertainty is certain, outcome will be new and new is always exiting.
I fear failure	There is no existence of failure. It is the learning to change the track and to decide where not to go

Bending the negative emotions to fruitfulness
Despite attempts, negative emotions may always exist, but you can negotiate with these adopting a clever way to deceive the negative force. Weird circuitry of your brain is accustomed to spot short term benefit easily than the effect in long term (discussed later in Hyperbolic discounting); similarly while aligning towards negative forces, it seems alluring as it has obvious short run fruit. However, it is possible to achieve desirable mind bend towards positive alignment camouflaged in negative traits. Lets have a look.

Don't delay in action but delay the gratification
Delay is always detrimental to progress, but for gratification you require procrastination of the enjoying fruits of short term achievement. Put your hardest effort first; let the foundation stone be laid stronger. If you give less priority for gratification, you save time to move your essential activity to complete. Early complacence not only kills times but creates a comfort zone for you which resist changes and drains your energy level which is required to be in full brim up to end.

Don't fear to change but fear the timeline
Change is never fateful; however, it is always resisted to remain in present comfort zone. Resisting change is linked with comfort as it is can avoid fear of uncertainty. But fact is that nothing in this world keeps constancy; for keeping pace with the time you have to embrace change coping up with new situation. You may forget the underlying truth that, remaining in one position does not assure you

guarantee to reap same benefit from your present comfort zone. Thus you need to visualize the new scenario and whatever change is beneficial to you should be readily accepted. Timely action to accept change is equally important for timely achievement and accelerated progress.

Don't repent on your fruitless action, but repent on your inaction
Fruitless action is like a bubble in the glass of water, allow it is to release through top. If you repent, it suppresses and it does not eliminate, it will tend to get bigger merging many bubbles together. Instead, repent on your inaction to find out ways getting out of it.

Don't get angry on criticism; get angry on your inability to keep cool
Criticism is the thorn in the bed of roses; it is unavoidable. People have tendency to discourage you by temping the short term happiness and by making you refrain from hard work. It gives people satisfaction as it reduces the chance of your attaining goal, which most of the people desired but not attained due to their lack of willingness to exert them. People may even criticize on your face and back if you try and laugh at if you fail. The laugh can only satisfy the criticizer (ref: verification supportive bias).

Therefore the criticism should not make you angry. Divert your disgust or anger on why you cannot keep your cool. It will trigger your cognitive brain to switch on to logical mode. You find easier way to keep your cool as the root cause of producing anger is eliminated with the help of logical mind overpowering the emotion.

Don't be selfish to deprive others but be selfish to get rid of your own comfort zone

Attaining any colossal achievement should not make you selfish as you would get detached from the people around you, your peer and friends, near and dear ones. Divert your self-centeredness inward instead of outward; getting rid of your own comfort zone. Then you will comfortably see other's interest in achieving your goal.

.

Don't be emotional but act with emotion

Emotion as we have seen blocks the logic during critical moments. The decision must be taken at cognitive brain, putting the logic in foremost position however the emotion or feeling of the heart is essentially required at back of mind for giving desired impetus. Thus your path to success will be guided by logic with certainty an emotional push from behind will prevent roll back, in case of negotiating steep slope of resistance. Emotion must push your logical decision towards goal but must not pull the decision towards diversions which is easy but likely to get lost. Dissociate emotion from response mechanism and attach to the action for implementation.

Optimizing positive energy with negative energy

We are already aware that negative emotions are much stronger than positive ones, as nature has designed the negative emotions for using as tools during survival need which demands sudden full surge of energy to combat with animosity. On the flip side positive energy flows slowly and it sometimes gets lost due to lack of impetus. Therefore, negative emotion like anger and disgust which are prominent negative emotions can be used as tools for imparting momentum. Positive logic with a tinge of negative emotion gives rise to a lethal combination, which are being used by top achievers for keeping the drive unperturbed.

CHAPTER-10

Fighting myths, paradoxes- a mathematical approach

"Scientific views end in awe and mystery, lost at the edge in uncertainty, but they appear to be so deep and so impressive that the theory that it is all arranged as a stage for God to watch man's struggle for good and evil seems inadequate."-**Richard P. Feynman**

"The concept of randomness and coincidence will be obsolete when people can finally define a formulation of patterned interaction between all things within the universe." -**Toba Beta**

Let me begin with a true story how a myth was basted with counteractive false belief. One of my childhood friends, Tapan had experimented healing of an acute mental problem in a teenage girl, who was happened to be his niece. She was not only having superstitions of many things including belief in existence of ghost but also having strong belief on every myth that persisted around her. Around 1988, she had once suspected by her parents to be tormented by a ghost, while she had gone to a particular pond at 12 noon, which was believed to be haunted at that time. When she was brought to Tapan, she was completely besieged and violently moving her head and found with locked jaw. Having his prior knowledge about her false belief and that of people around her, he at first gained her confidence by telling the other people that he understood she had been besieged by ghost. The trick worked fine as she eavesdropped to the statement and believed that Tapan has the capability of detecting the ghost within her. She had naturally believed that the person who can exorcise the ghost must have the capability to detect it.

Tapan reinforced her belief in same method, elaborately describing to people gathered around her how he got one impeccable weapon which can definitely drag the ghost out of her. Then he turned her false belief to positive direction by describing the past experience of 100% success of that tool (although Tapan had no previous experience actually) applied on other persons.

He used the weird trick, generally adopted by so called ghost busters, telling her she would get a great jolt when she touches that thing (a small metal piece posed as sacred weapon) and stubborn ghost would have no option but to come out from her body. Her belief at that moment was so strong on her uncle; she finally mimicked a jolt as a reaction to his weird trick and actually fainted thereafter. When she regained consciousness, she became normal as before.

Counter-intuitive approach helps busting myths and building up logical understanding of the events. We generally, tend to infer conclusion from our own intuition, whereas reality can differ much from what we presume. The myths we tend to believe is a form of negative intuition but can be combated effectively by positive logic only. Some of the paradoxes like The Monty Hall problem and Birthday paradox are illustrated here to explain that there is greater chance of occurrence of an event than what we think intuitively. Uncertain outcome can be ascertained more precisely in a probabilistic scenario, if we put the things together in order of logical sequence.

We get confused easily to decide what to choose out of multiple choices, like choosing an eatery for mid-day meal in a strange locale or deciding menu for family or may be choosing a cab to go far. Especially decision making process seems more complex when comparable attributes are hard to differentiate. Most of the choices we encounter in life are not fully exclusive, but on the contrary, they are dependent on other factors which are not in our full control. The factors govern the likelihood of occurring the desired outcomes are called 'conditions' and the possibility of happening under the given condition is termed as conditional probability.

Let us understand with a practical example,

Probabilities of life events are not merely a chance but depend on sincere efforts put in and are pivotal on subjective viewpoint.

Suppose you have decided to raise your son to become a doctor. Your decision is dependent on the success of following realistic (say mutually exclusive as well) events:

Chance that you are married to a fertile wife (say 95% likely)

Chance that your wife and you have no limitation to give birth sufficient no of child until arrival of son (say 90% likely)

Chance that your son is survived upto an minimum age of say, 22 (say 95% likely).

 Chance that he is brilliant enough to get through exams or gets admission by other means (say 90% likely).

Chance that your son completes the course (say 95% likely).

So the probability that your son becomes a doctor as per rationalistic estimation= Probability of having a son, provided that you marry to a fertile wife having fair chance of giving birth a male child and provided that your son is enough brilliant and subsequently completes the course   =P(A)XP(B)XP(C)XP(D)XP(E) =95%X90%X95%X90%X95% =69.4%

Now let us understand what statistics call as conditional probability and the implication to our belief and superstition.

It is evident that the ultimate probability of becoming your son a doctor depends on a series of successful events which should happen in chronological succession and some are mutually exclusive in timeline. At any stage of event, if failure occurs the ultimate probability will turn out to be zero. Some of the event carries binary possibilities at certain stage, such as P(A)= wife may be fertile or infertile; P(B)= wife may give birth to son or daughter; Survival of son, P(C)=he may be alive or dead up to certain time etc. On the other side probabilities of happening to you or particular person may not be 0.5 even possibilities are binary. Rather, most of the events are dependent on personal efforts while a few of them are not controllable by putting effort or corrective actions.

Such as, P(A)=if wife found infertile it may or may not be corrected. You cannot control birth of son, hence to be accepted as happened.

Some of the events like probability of getting through entrance and successful completion of course can be improved by proper action which depends on various conditions.

Now let us understand what optimists and pessimists are thinking about ultimate probability of above problem.

Optimized Optimist thinks probability of events with binary possibilities is 100% which means outcome will be favourable, thus P(A), P(B), P(C) all will have 100% probability. For them ultimate probability will be =100%X100%X100%X90%X95%= 85.5%

On the contrary, optimized pessimist will incorporate a subjective probability (chance that he would put his best effort in every step) to rational estimate of likelihood; namely 69.4%XP(subj)=69.4%X(say80%, based on data of ratio of no of person attempted to population having opportunity)=55.5%.

For pure pessimist the ultimate probability will be zero as one or more of the components are thought by them to be zero.

The probabilities thus vary depending upon how the happenings are viewed from different perspectives. Majority of real events are having conditional on other factors. Conditional probabilities may be understood through Bayes' theorem which underlines hypothesis and evidences.

Conditional Probabilities and Bayes' theorem

Conditional probability is the probability of occurring an event or hypothesis conditional on another event or evidence.

Suppose the probability of H (hypothesis) is conditional on E (evidence) is PE(H)

Unconditional Probability of hypothesis and evidence is P(H & E)

And unconditional probability of evidence is P(E), then according to Bayes theorem,

PE(H) = P(H & E)/P(E), provided that both terms of this ratio exist and P(E) > 0

Let's illustrate with a test scenario where you are detected positive with enlarged prostate and your logical reaction should be how is probability of having this, even if you have been tested positive.

If we put the above theorem into a practical example the scenario will be like illustration 1 as given below.

Illustration 1: Positive test results do not mean anyone is actually carrying disease

A.Say, 1.5% of men in entire population of men have enlarged prostate, which is denoted by P(A) and therefore 98.5% do not have, say P(~A).

B.Say, 85% of UT report detect enlarged prostate when it is really there (and therefore 15% report will miss it even if it is there), say P(X|A). If you already have enlarged prostate, it means there's an 85% chance you will test positive in UT report. There's a 15% chance you will test negative.

C.Say, 8% of UT report detects enlarged prostate when it's not there (and therefore 92% correctly return a negative result), say. P(X|~A). If you don't have enlarged prostate, there's an 8% chance you will test positive, and a 92% chance you will test negative.

D.The chance of getting any type of positive result = the chance of a true positive plus the chance of a false positive, say P(X).

E.We would like to know the chance of having enlarged prostate even if test indicates positive, say P(A|X)

Now let us determine the scenario based on test accuracy (< 100%)

•The test which detected the prostate enlargement correctly is termed as true positive and the test when detects wrongly even if you don't have any is false positive.

• Then the chances of a true positive = probability of having enlarged prostate X chance test detect it = 1.5% * 85% = .01277, say 0.013

•The chances of a false positive = Probability that you don't have enlarged prostate X chance test detect it anyway = 98.5% * 8% = 0.0788

We will try to find out what's the chance you really have enlarged prostate if you get a positive result. The chance of an event is the number of ways it could happen given all possible outcomes:

Probability = desired event / all possible outcome

The chance of getting a real, positive result is .013. The chance of getting any type of positive result is the chance of a true positive plus the chance of a false positive (0.013 + 0.0788 = .0918), {P(X)}.

So, our chance of enlarged prostate is (chance of getting a true positive result)/ (chance of getting any type of positive result)=0.013/.0918 = 0.1416, or about 14.16% only.

That is how it is interesting that a positive UT report only means you have a 14.16% chance of enlarged prostate, rather than 85% (the supposed accuracy of the test). Hence the actual chance is counter intuitive, i.e. it far less than what our intuition dictates us.

If we go with Bayes theorem then $P(A|X) = P(X|A)*P(A)/P(X)$

$=0.85*0.015/0.0908=0.1416=14.16\%$

The catch: Don't go by intuition, whenever you are prone to have negative impact on your thought, think rational.

So now what will be your rational decision? Should you think this 14.16% chance of having to take it as false positive with certainty? Or you take another test to other laboratory and repeat test on same laboratory.

Let's assume accuracy of test in labs is unknown and tests are done at random.

Illustration2: Repeat the doubted test (false positive) in same lab rather than choosing another.

Probability of false positive if test is carried out in same laboratory

The chances of a false positive = Probability that you don't have enlarged prostate X chance that test detects it anyway = 98.5% * 8% = 0.0788

Probability of repeat test report coming out as false positive in same laboratory is

98.5%* 8%*8%=. 0.0063

Probability if test is carried out in different laboratory

The chances of a false positive in one lab = the chances of a false positive in another lab =Probability that you don't have enlarged prostate X chance test detect it anyway = 98.5% * 8% = 0.0788

Therefore, it is counter-intuitive fact that you should go in for a repeat test in same lab to reduce the chance of false positive report, than to test in a different lab. Therefore second test in same lab may have fairer chance of true positive or true negative and considered as true report whatever the result may be.

The catch: Even first test has come out as false positive in first lab, the probability of repeat test coming out as false positive is less in first lab than that of test carried out in any other lab.

Illustration 3: Chance (of ill luck) is much less than you think: Sick Child and Doctor.

A doctor is to see a sick child who has prior information that 90% of sick children in that area have the flu, and rest (10%) is suffering from measles.

Let F is denoted by an event of a child being sick with flu and M represents event of a child being sick with measles. It is assumed that no child is suffering from both the disease, i.e. events F and M are mutually exclusive (FUM = Ω), i.e., there is no other disease prevailing in children of that area.

In general, patient suffering from measles develop outward symptom, skin rash, which may be denoted as R. The probability of skin rash, given that it is from measles is P(R|M) = 0.95.

Occasionally children with flu also develop skin rash, thus event of rash being developed by flu is P(R|F) = 0.08.

Now the question is what is the probability that child is suffering from measles? P(M|R)=P(R|M)XP(M)/{P(R|M)XP(M)+P(R|F)XP(F)}

=.95X0.10/(.95X0.10+0.08X.90)=0.57

Therefore it is far less (57%) than what is thought (95%) to actual by intuition.

Illustration 4: The Chance is fairer than you think: Monty Hall Problem

The Monty hall problem was named after a American TV game show, where participants are given the choice of three doors: Behind one door is a car; behind the other two, goats. Suppose anyone choose a door, say No. 1, and the host, who knows what is behind which door, opens another door, say No. 2, which reveals a goat. Then he says "Do you want to change your choice to door No. 3?"

What will be the right decision, to stick to original choice or to change to another?

The answer will be: changing the original option will have greater chance to win. Let us explain how it can be possible to get chances to win fairer.

There are 2 goats out of 3 doors. Thus, players initially have a 2/3 chance picking a goat.

Those who swap choice will always get the opposite of their original choice.

Therefore, players who always swap have a 2/3 chance of getting the car.

Paradoxial, isn't it?

+	Behind Door 1	Behind Door2	Behind Door3	Outcome if staying with original choice (door-1)	Outcome if choice is swapped (door-2or 3)
Opt-1	Car	Goat (host reveals)	Goat	Car	Goat

Opt-2	Goat	Car	Goat(host reveals)	Goat	Car
Opt-3	Goat	Goat (host reveals)	Car	Goat	Car
Probability of out come to be Car				1/3	2/3

The above answer depends on the following criteria:

The host is to always reveal a goat.

He must know beforehand what is behind which door.

We might analyze exhaustive outcomes behind each door and if choice is swapped, probability of car behind the door will become 2/3 instead of original 1/3.

Therefore choosing the favourable door is not much difficult than we think they would be.

Illustration 5: Task is much easier thank you think: Birthday Paradox

Let us discuss about one more paradox which is also counterintuitive.

Birthday Paradox: Only 23 people are required to make 50-50 chance of two people having same birthday. If sample size is 75 persons, the chance raised to 99.9%.

Brush up text book knowledge of combination and permutation and Let's see why the paradox happens and how it works.

With 23 people we have 253 pairs: {(23X22)/2}

The chance of 2 people having different birthdays is:

1-1/365=364/365=0.997260

The probability of 2 people having different birthdays in 253 pair= (364/365)253=0.4995=49.95%

The chance that we have a pair of 2 people having same birthday is: 1 – 49.95% = 50.05%.

If no. of people is raised to 75, we have 75X74/2= 2775 pairs

The probability of 2 people having different birthdays in 2775 pair= (364/365) 2775 =0.00049=0.049%

The chance that we have a pair of 2 people having same birthday is: 1 – 0.049%= 99.95%. Therefore there is almost certain that we will find a pair of persons with same birthday amongst 73 people.

The Catch: Intuition cannot understand proportions by which likelihood is raised.

Illustration 6: It is possible to turn ill-luck into your fortune: Parrondo's paradox

This is a paradox in game theory, describes as: The strategies which are losing strategies in isolation are combined together in certain manner, may form a winning strategy. It was created by, Juan Parrondo, who discovered the paradox in 1996. The paradox is comprehensively described as:

There exist pairs of games, each with a higher probability of losing than winning, for which it is possible to construct a winning strategy by playing the games alternately.

In connection with the analysis of the Brownian ratchet by Parrondo, a thought experiment of a machine able to extract energy from random heat motions, which was originally conceived by physicist Richard Feynman, was the precursor of discovery of this paradox.

Let us consider an example how and why the paradox works. Consider two games **Game A** and **Game B**, with the following rules:

1.In **Game A**, you lose 100% of the time, losing Rs1 each time you play

2.In **Game B**, you count how much money you have left. If it's a multiple of 5, then you win Rs 6. If it's not, then you lose Rs. 4.

Playing Game A alone is a losing strategy, since you lose every time you play.

Playing Game B alone is also a losing strategy, since you will lose four out of every five times you play, thus losing Rs.16 for every Rs.6 you win, for an average net loss of Rs. 2 per game.

However if Games A and B are played in alternating sequence of one game of A followed by one game of B (A,B,A,B,A,B), then you will win in the long run, because the first time you play Game B with a remaining balance that is a multiple of 5, you will win Rs.6, then play Game A and lose Rs.1, and play Game B again with exactly Rs.5

more, i.e. you will continue to win Game B indefinitely, accumulating Rs.5 each time (Rs6-Rs.1).

Application: Parrondo's paradox is used extensively in game theory, and its application in engineering, population dynamics, financial risk, etc., Simple finance textbook models of security returns have been used to prove that individual investments with negative median long-term returns may be easily combined into diversified portfolios with positive median long-term returns.

Probabilistic approach in Progressive Visualization- Role of Bayes' Theorem

Subjective probability theory highlights evidential support by which anyone learns to develop perception about what is likely and what is not.

According to Bayesian theory the guideline parameters are:

Confirmational relativity

Relationship between evidence and hypothesis are obviously relativistic upon individual and their degree of belief which is called *Confirmational Relativity*. It means a hypothesis may be perceived as truth is dependent on individual degree of belief. No of evidences required by one person for hypothesis to be truth may be greater than number of the same by another person.

Suppose a heart surgeon which was earlier unknown to you and the residents of that locality. You are required to recommend someone for a by-pass surgery of heart. You gathered data about past success rate of that surgeon. You came to know that no of last consecutive successful operation were 12, before that 15 operation went wrong out of 25 operations carried out in his career. Your belief that the doctor has gained sufficient knowledge of by-pass surgery will get stronger with no successive successful operation in later stage. Suppose, you observed he has carried out 3 more operations which went consecutively successful, you became fully confident on that doctor. But your friend might have already believed after 2 operations that the doctor is reliable. Thus the confirmational evidence required by one person differs from another person.

Evidence proportionism

Rationality can be introduced in proportionate confidence depending upon the evidence in support of a hypothesis. Rational believer proportions his or her confidence in a hypothesis H to his or her total evidence for H. Subjective probability for H reflects the overall balance of his/her reasons for or against its truth.

Say, you came to know about a belief that whenever a cat crosses someone's way he or she will encounter danger or failure very soon. You being a rational observer observed the event occurred several times say 20 times, and you came across unexpected failure or danger in 2 occasions. Your confidence in belief of the hypothesis that crossing cat indicates upcoming danger is 2/20, i.e. 1% only.

Incremental confirmation

The set of data to the extent which provides incremental evidence in support of hypothesis, H to raise its probability is called incremental confirmation. Suppose, hypothesis that white crow is non-existent in the earth has the probability P(H)=30% given that 60 countries explored out of 195 countries in the world. It has later observed after 50% of ocean area, white crow is non-existent. The probability P(H) gets more than 90% incorporating ocean data, thereby provides incremental confirmation to the probability.

It is indicative from the above statements about evidentiary relationships always make implicit reference to people and their degrees of belief. Therefore, "E is evidence for H" should really be read as "E is evidence for H with reference to information implied in the subjective probability P".

Right mix of data and intuitive thoughts

Need is felt to use right mix of statistics and intuitive actions as everyday life will turn out to be a complex mathematical lab if we calculate probabilities for evading intuition in each and every small decision. Mathematical modelling is only to give a treat to mind so that intuition would not be path blocker to your decision making process and it would make process moderately rational by triggering cognitive brain to take control. It is not intended to make each and every decision by analyzing statistical data such as going for a vacation, searching restaurant etc., whereas only a phone call or reading review from web would be useful to make fair judgment. Counter intuitive approach should be used as tools to fight intuitive thought that hinders your progress especially when large impacts on behavioural or financial matters are imminent.

I would suggest cognitive mind set is to be used to ascertain where to use the intuition and where to use statistics rather than intuition itself to decide the same.

CHAPTER-11

Optimal Decision making under uncertainty

"Without the element of uncertainty, the bringing off of even, the greatest business triumph would be dull, routine, and eminently unsatisfying."-**J. Paul Getty**

"A good decision cannot guarantee a good outcome. All real decisions are made under uncertainty. A decision is therefore a bet, and evaluating it as good or not must depend on the stakes and the odds, not on the outcome."-**Ward Edwards**

With the advancement of knowledge of cognitive science, we came to know that numerous mental habits and biases are affecting our optimal and rational decision making processes, thereby necessitates controlling these barriers so that we can become better-decision makers to achieve our goals more often in all spheres of life. However, decision making process under uncertainty is still a complex process as all decision making barriers like intuitions; gut feelings, judgmental biases etc are difficult to rule out. Statistical approach resolved this to some extent, which helps us unfocus the decision criteria on subjective judgment and views the probability of outcomes in certain possible scenarios, based on which decision under uncertainty is founded.

Classical statistical methods employ theoretical approach for sampling of population and its characteristics. Modern statistical approach helps generate and chose various options and the consequences and present optimal decision we should go in for; in this manner, it guides us to take optimal decision under uncertainty.

In order to ascertain best suitable alternatives under uncertainties, statistics employ a loss function or reward function and further determines expected minimum loss or maximum reward. For easier understanding, one parameter i.e. loss function may be taken for calculation. The value of the loss function itself is a random quantity because it depends on the outcome of a random variable X, which can be ascertained in both Frequentist and Bayesian method.

Frequentist expected loss

It is expressed as risk function $R(\theta, \delta)$, where θ is state of the nature and δ is decision rule, having expected loss $L(\theta, \delta(x))$ with respect to the probability distribution, $P\theta$, of the observed data, X under decision rule δ and the parameter θ. The risk function is given as $R(\theta,\delta)=\int L(\theta, \delta(x)) \, dP\theta(x)$

Bayesian expected loss

In a Bayesian approach, the loss function is derived using the Posterior Distribution π of the parameter. Posterior probability accounts for prior occurrences of events and its probability. Posterior probability with respect to observation of $x = P(\theta \mid x) = \{P(x \mid \theta) \times P(\theta)\}/P(x)$.

Where $P(\theta \mid x)$ is the probability of θ with respect to X

Where P(x | θ) is the probability of X with respect to θ

According to Bayesian method loss function ρ (π, a) =∫ θ L (θ, a) d π (θ) Thus risk is entirely based on θ. In order to take an optimal decision, we have to adopt best risk estimator. Here are two estimators which reduces risk in various forms.

Least maximum risk estimator: In frequentist framework, estimator which derives least value of risk for all values of θ, it is called minimax (least maximum loss scenario) principle.

Bayesian Risk estimator: Risk can also be minimized following Bayesian method by minimizing average risk with respect to prior π to θ. It means, estimator minimizes average risks considering data prior to occurrence of θ are being evaluated.

In both the methods, we are to determine and choose action 'a' which is having minimum expected loss. Although this will result in choosing the same action as would be chosen using the Bayes risk, Bayesian approach underlines in choosing the optimal action under the actual observed data. Bayes optimal decision rule, is a function of all possible observational data, thus poses a much more difficult problem in computation.

We may compute required parameters based on frequentist approach in simplest form. First of all let's introduce three important parameters namely:

State of nature (θ): It is termed as possible input parameter which forces us to decide our action, such as grabbing an opportunity to change job, to buy an apartment, to quit a bad habit, to adopt a child or to get a divorce.

Decision Space, d(X): It expresses all possible values of decision parameter, such as

Loss function, L: It determines consequential losses involved in each set of decision parameter. $L(\theta, d(X))$ based on worst case scenario.

Risk, R $(\theta, d(x))$: It determines risk involved in particular decision under certain state of nature.

Let us illustrate an example on decision making if cloudburst is likely in hilly area.

Suppose State of the nature

$\theta = 0$ means "No cloudburst at hill"
$\theta = 1$ means "Cloudburst at hill"
Then Decision Space, D(x) will be like this
0=Stay in foothills

1=leave foothills

Loss Function in worst case scenario will be:

$L(0,0) = 0$
$L(0,1) = $ cost of moving
$L(1,1) = $ cost of moving + cost of belongings we cannot move
$L(1,0) = $ loss of belongings + loss of life
Risk function will be:
R $(0,0)=$ No risk
R $(0,1)=$No risk
R $(1,1)=$ No risk
R $(1,0)=$ Risk of endangering life

The above equations explicitly have taken into consideration the maximum risk involved based on worst case criteria. However there is possibility that each cloudburst is not having the risk of flooding the foothills, so that inhabitants have to move out.

In a real case of natural disaster of Hurrycane in Odisha (Phailin) we may analyze risk functions in light of statistical approach.

Case 2: Evacuation in Phailin Hurrycane in 2013

Statistical parameters of the real scenario will be like this:
State of the nature
$\theta = 0$ means "No Cyclone to hit east coast"
$\theta = 1$ means "Cyclone to hit east coast"
Decision Space is like this
D (0,1)= D(Stay in muddy houses, leave for far-off places)

Scenario	Loss function	Risk function	View point
1.Cyclone diverted, stay in coast	L(0,0) = 0	R (0,0)= No risk	Rational
2.Cyclone diverted, still leave coastal line	L(0,1) = cost of evacuation	R (0,1)=No risk	Pessimistic
3.Cyclone hit coast, leave coastal line	L(1,1) = cost of evacuation + cost of property damage	R (1,1)= No risk	Rational
4.Cyclone hit coast, stay in coastal line	L(1,0) = loss of belongings + loss of life	R (1,0)= Risk of endangering life	Optimistic

Leaving apart the above analysis, learning lesson from the 1999 super cyclone in Odisha, although does not signify Bayesian learning process, but emphasizes learning of key parameters of effective disaster management. The sea monster of 2013 could have run havoc if government would not take timely and heroic action evacuating lacs of people from the coastal area.

With muddy and thatched houses along sea coast, nothing would have been a better option rather than choosing options for evacuating millions of people for saving lives. Technology helped predicting speed and locus of the cyclone, resulted in minute-by-minute broadcast about the onset of the same; It was lot easier to understand where it would have land fall and by what time. We knew that loss of properties is unavoidable, as they are not provided with proper housing which could withstand at least 200 kmph wind speed.

Now, the question is what decision criteria had been adopted to evacuate two lac people within short notice of nearly 48 hours?

It was obviously prudent to adopt rational criteria where minimum loss without endangering life (scenario3) is involved. The decision has been backed by correct identification of target people with the help of advanced meteorological forecast, thus decision criteria was optimized with the help of technology. It underlines the fact, wherever statistical optimization is not so fruitful due to lack of prior data, technology may help us to arrive optimized pessimistic approach. Optimization was inevitable as time was short, and with reasonable amount of prediction accuracy, location of land fall was known. Therefore target people had been identified with much accuracy who had to leave the coastal line.

If question arises what could have been much better if we learnt from the past or even for future what decision criteria will save not only lives but also save properties and underlying huge cost of evacuation and rehabilitation—probably building proper housing for the residents of coastal people defying the ravages of sea. Is it a distant dream?

Case-2: Now let us discuss about a hypothetical case in which quantifiable historical data is available to analyze for forecasting expectations in future outcome.

Analysis of possible scenario

When we go with certain decision, it calls for crosschecking the impact of implementation of the same. We may consider four aspects, most optimistic, worst case (pessimistic), most likely scenario and most optimum. Analysis between these scenarios may reach you finalizing the decision which may be resorted with a view to minimize risk or to maximize potential etc.

Let us illustrate this with an example:

XYZ fertilizer ltd is producing a special type of chemical fertilizer, neem coated urea having production capacity of 500000 MT, over the year. This special fertilizer is sold Rs. 4000 a metric ton (MT) and the firm incurs Rs 3500 per MT; when it is unsold, over the winter; it has to recycle back into its partial process and incurs Rs 100 per ton. The firm must, therefore, decide what the most economic production quantity is before winter. Comparing 5 years` records, the following data on annual sales:

History of Sales (MT)	Years of Given Sales
100000	0
200000	1
300000	1
400000	2
500000	1

We are to determine the production figures based on the following criteria:

a) How many MT of neem coated urea should be produced by XYZ fertilizer ltd may be based on past sales figure.

b) Production figure would minimize the recycle so that additional cost of recycle is least incurred.

c) Decision making will occur within a risk environment (based on the fact that past records have provided a probability distribution of annual sales).

Criteria Establishment

Let us define a "decision criterion" as an indicator for measuring the objective. Our objective is to find proper production figure under the following assumptions:

M/s XYZ fertilizer produces and delivers completely whatever market demand is.

M/s XYZ fertilizer want to minimize recycle to minimize additional cost in long run.

It may be observed that selection of a decision criterion involves a subjective judgment, which is short term in nature. Therefore, to arrive at decision as per long term objective, common decision criteria may be:

a) Maximum absolute gain-Optimistic scenario.

b) Maximum expected gain-optimized optimistic scenario.

c) Minimum expected loss-.optimized pessimistic scenario

d) Minimum absolute loss -Pessimistic or worst case scenario.

<u>Maximum Absolute Gain</u> is a decision criterion generally selected through optimistic view. This criterion keeps in view amount of gross profits associated with each alternative and dictates the selection of production figure irrespective of the probability of attaining that profit. If decision maker of XYZ fertilizer is an optimist and selects the Maximum Absolute Gain criterion, his resulting decision would be to produce 500000 MT of Neem coated fertilizer (Table 2). In case, demands that year was 500000 MT, he would receive the maximum absolute gross profit of Rs 25 Cr. Manager of XYZ fertilizer, who is optimist in all cases would make this decision despite the fact that there is only a 20 per cent likelihood that his annual sales will reach 500000 tons neem coated urea, i.e., only in one year of the past 5 year the demand has reached that level.

Table2: Decision criterion-1: Max Absolute Gross Gain

Maximum Absolute Potential Demand (MT)	Gross Profit Per (MT)	Total Absolute Gross Gain
100000	Rs 500	Rs 5 Cr.
200000	Rs 500	Rs 10 Cr
300000	Rs 500	Rs 15 Cr
400000	Rs 500	Rs 20 Cr
500000	Rs 500	Rs 25 Cr

Table3: Decision criterion-2: Maximum Expected Gross Gain

Annual Demand (MT)	Probability of Demand Occurring	Total Absolute Gross Gain	Expected Gross Gain (col2Xcol3)
200000	.20	Rs 10 cr	Rs. 2 cr
300000	.20	Rs 15 cr	Rs. 3 cr.
400000	.40	Rs 20 cr	Rs. 6 cr
500000	.2	Rs 25 cr	Rs 5 cr.
	1.00		

Table4: Decision criterion-3: Minimum Expected Loss

		Annual Demand			
		200000	300000	400000	500000
Probability of Demand D	D= prodn	.20	.20	.40	.20
	D< Prodn	0	.20	.40	.80
	D> prodn	.80	.60	.20	0

Expec ted	Loss due to Unsold stock	0	500(0.2* 100000)	500(0.2* 200000+ 0.2* 100000)	500(0.2* 300000+.2* 200000+.4* 100000)
	Overstock Opport. Cost	0	100(0.2* 100000).	100(0.2* 200000+ 0.2* 100000)	100(0.2* 300000+.2* 200000+.4* 100000).
	Under stock Opportun e cost	500(0.2 * 100000 +0.4* 200000 +0.2* 300000)	500(0.4* 100000+0 .2* 200000)	500(0.2* 100000)	0
Total Expected loss		Rs 8cr	Rs5.2 cr	Rs 4.6 Cr	Rs 8 Cr.

Minimum Absolute Loss on worst case scenario takes into account the absolute magnitude of likely losses and chooses the minimum value. Under this criterion, a decision maker will minimize loss if the worst possible event (in this case a demand of only 200000 MT) occur as his decision are based on "avoid risk" philosophy. This criterion does not cover any possibility of occurrence of losses.

Table5: Decision criterion-4: Min. Absolute Loss w.r.t. worst case scenario

Annual Demand	Cost of Unsold Fertilizer	Worst Overstock Opportunity Cost	Worst Possible Understock Opportunity Cost	Total Absolute Loss
2,00,000	0	0	Rs500* 300000	Rs15 cr
3,00,000	Rs.500* 100000	Rs100* 100000	Rs 500* 200000	Rs16 cr
4,00,000	Rs. 500* 200000	Rs100* 200000	Rs 500* 100000	Rs17 cr
5,00,000	Rs. 500X* 300000	Rs100* 300000	0	Rs18 cr

<u>Maximum Expected Net Value</u>: Considering limitations of all 4 criteria a fifth decision criteria has been evolved through development of statistics, wherein maximum expected net value (expected value of profit-expected value of losses)

This criterion keeps all possible elements of the problem in view and may be the most comprehensive measure for decision under uncertainty. Under this criterion, the expected net value of the example can be computed as follows:

Managerial Actions on production (tons)	Expected profit	Expected loss	Expected net value
200000	Rs. 2 cr	Rs 8cr	-6
300000	Rs. 3 cr.	Rs5.2cr	-2.2
400000	Rs. 6 cr	Rs4.6cr	+1.4
500000	Rs 5 cr.	Rs8.4cr	-3.4

Based on the above five criteria of decision making we get different decision alternative having potential of producing best result under various uncertainties. Since Uncertainties are really unpredictable, the decision which accounts for maximizing expected profit and minimizing expected loss by the parameter expected net value would be best possible alternative for truly unpredictable scenario.

Deriving the decision makers Trait

If we put all possible mind sets of decision makers w.r.t. their decision making traits, we may arrive on what could be the most gainful criteria.

Table-7 Decision maker's trait

	Criterion 1	Criterion 2	Criterion 3	Criterion 4	Criterion 5
	Maximum Absolute Gross Gain	Maximum Expected Gross Gain	Minimum Expected Loss	Minimum Absolute Loss	Maximum Expected Net Value Alternatives
Amount	50000	40000	40000	20000	40000
trait	Optimist	Optimized optimist	Optimized pessimist	pessimist	Rationalist

From the above comparison, it is evident that optimal criteria for decision are either optimized optimist or optimized pessimist (although outcome is happened to be similar to that of Rational criteria) which is most likely to maximize expected profit or minimize expected loss, as the case may be.

CHAPTER 12

Handling hypothetical and self linked biases

"If my theory of relativity is proven successful, Germany will claim me as a German and France will declare me that I am a citizen of world. Should my theory prove untrue, France will say that I am a German and Germany will declare that I am a Jew" **–Albert Einstein**

In July 2012, violence at Manesar plant of Maruti Suzuki was spread out, where one HR manager was killed and subsequently it was revealed that the truth was contrived as being told to outer world simply as 'Murderous workers' vs. 'Rational management'. There was obvious reason behind the violence and that was extreme exploitation of workers and disproportionate reward to their work.

The facts came out to expose following 'out of proportion' parameters:

3. Company's profit goes up 2200% over nine years.

4. CEO's pay goes up by 419% over four years.

5. CEO's gets Rs 20Lacs per month while a permanent worker get max Rs17000/-.

6. Workers wage increase in four years by 5.5% against consumer price index of 50% against 2007 data.

7. Workers get 7.5 min tea/toilet break in 8 hour. He is supposed to run 150 meter to pick up tea and snack and run another 400 meter for toilet holding the tea snack, eats snacks while in toilet, otherwise he can lose half-a-day salary.

8. Worker can lose nearly half his salary for taking a couple of days leave in a month.

The company blames labour laws: Company find difficult to follow those laws as there are about 55 central labour laws and more than a 100 state laws and even these laws creates difficulty to lay off a worker, led to situation where company hires majority of contract labour.

(Source: Article by G Sampath: Can India Inc. face the truth about the Manesar Violence?)

The above example illustrates a bias called Perceived credential bias which pertains to credential of an individual or group of individuals about taking the credit or putting the blame for action which has already taken place and is difficult to prove in normative approach, whoever is actually responsible. The bias has also been utilized in wrong way, when affected individual or group are unsuspicious or unaware that they are being used up or falling prey to it. Similar case in general may prevail in large vertical organizations, wherein particular group of people work for self satisfaction and self motivation may not get justified and proportionate reward as credit goes to manager who works without any value addition or significant contribution. The overutilization of bias, ultimately create awareness in long run among people who are affected, sometimes results in extreme dissatisfaction and ultimate disaster.

There are others, which may pose threat to individual or group of people.

Low intensity corporate bias

Besides the extreme level of bias as illustrated above, there may be low key bias which is prevailed over very long time and formed as a corporate culture, creating low intensity dissatisfaction to most of the people but viewed as reasonable to few.

Example: In general, large chemical processing installation comprises of various disciplines, nevertheless, it is generally seen that production is deemed to be most important operation while in most of the cases maintaining the availability of equipments has the greatest impact on production; still it is seen as unreasonable parameter to improve sales or production.

Influencer: Influencers of this bias are mostly group of people who gets benefitted from the bias in terms of undue reward like pay hike etc.

Preventer: The affected people should take the initiative to clarify the bias with the evidences and logic. Repeated and multiple exposure to clarity will result in triggering 'evidence proportionism' effect in decision maker.

Idol worship bias

The bias is prevalent among followers of an influential person about fanfare and idol worshiping. The person may be from the film, politics, singer, dancer, sports or in spiritual sphere. In general, people fall in trap of this bias on their own, sometimes bias is purposely created by the influential person to get him advantages. In this bias people cannot see the dark side of his idol or turn a blind eye towards rational understanding about related events.

Example: It is prevalent that spiritual gurus are active in multiple domains. Most of them are imparting yoga classes; a few are also distributing unconventional medicine etc. Physical fitness or medicine shows its good effect on its own but the good effects are attributed to spiritual leader. In a peak of blindness, a follower attributes all good thing happened in his life to his blessings of guru and bad things to his luck.

Influencers: The lack of rationality and a common misbelief that our fate can be changed by someone else not by our will or hard work are the top influencers for this bias.

Preventer: It is very much true that there is no powerful person in the world who can change plight of common people unless we try to change ourselves.

Usage: The bias is used effectively in marketing and advertisement, wherein great personality endorses merchandise trying to influence people for buying the same.

Where to avoid: When the guru or his close disciples are endorsing products or imparting training, the blindness to faith is imparted. Suppose, a trainer of the guru says "you cannot reciprocate your learning to someone else on your own, we are only the authorized persons to impart training". The alarm should be raised as they're actually preachers in disguise of trainer.

Moral credential effect [j]

This bias occurs in a person, who has substantial track record as good egalitarian, generally forms an unconscious ethical endorsement within himself, which ultimately leads to erosion of principle within supporting environment and turn him to less egalitarian. The chance of being less egalitarian at later stage does not have any correlation with awareness or unawareness of peer group of that person.

Example: In case a person acts as sole financial decision maker, who has good track record in fair dealing, is likely to change himself to fit in unfair dealing, in future under certain circumstances.

The person who has favoured recruiting topers from the recognized institutes in the past more likely to favour recruiting less talented people at later stage.

A person who practiced moral or dignified action in terms of transparency and magnanimity in the past may get into corruption and discrimination.

Influencers: The unlimited power and sole authority for long time is identified as top influencer of this bias.

Preventer: Cross functional groups having shared responsibilities, audits from independent authority.

Cognitive Dissonance [a]

Feeling of conflicting thought arising from decision or action contrary to belief or self image is called cognitive dissonance. The situation aggravates with increase in intensity of thoughts due to its impact on how strongly it affects us socially, economically, physically. The action which initiates conflicting thoughts would result in change in behaviour, justifying the underlying decision or action by changing or modifying conflicting cognition.

The following example illustrates

Suppose anyone has changed the job for betterment of career, but find himself awkward in the new job and ultimately gets dissatisfied. He may find justification to appease self or peers by saying he changed the job due to better amenities available nearby.

Influencer: Negative thought of seeing dark side is the top influencer for this bias.

Preventer: Changed cognition, can help eliminate fear to changes. Moreover, he has to believe that change is the natural law of universe which is made for progress.

Bias Over disproportionate ego

It is just like "elephant may pass through small hole but its tail will stuck". We tend to see priority and importance of decision in terms of fulfilling our ego or mental satisfaction but not over the impact on end result. We negotiate heavily on small things of small value but for bigger objects of desire, we negotiate lightly or go after it easily, as it fulfils the desire more than its discount.

Example: We go for big investment or for building asset, purchasing high end properties, based on fulfilment of desire, we tend not to find alternative or invest in it on momentary decision, we are less likely to follow utilitarian approach. On the other hand, we keep on using old fashioned technology in consumer electronics like cell phone, PC, even if technology is fast changing allowing user to utilize more function with less difficulty.

Usage: Sales persons use this bias to motivate people for purchasing high value purchases like houses, high end cars, club memberships by symbolizing status statement for the user.

Where to avoid: At receiving end of the communication, you are required to consider the ground realities, capabilities commensurate to your spending.

Bias over persistence of feeling

It's not just about "First impression last forever" but it underlines importance of packaging a hard message inside positive transaction and finding secret within ulterior communication when you are at receiving end. Any prior statement that carries a positive or negative message shall persist over subsequent message that carries opposite impact. The receiver gets biased over the first impression of the message which is able to eclipse the ill effect of the concealed message in the subsequent statement or entire message which is intended to convey.

Example: CEO of an organization says to its executives, "You are one of the gems in this industry for which the company has come to this point. But it's a fact, the company is going through bad patches and not meeting bottom line. It is our responsibility to turn the company to right path; there is no end of improvement. You are the capable people who can introspect on your own to find out what are the shortcomings in you and I am sure you can find before others tell you".

Usage: The bias is primarily used to motivate people with good words carrying the right message, pointing out how to find shortcomings, but certainly not covering what exactly the deficiencies are. Even in case of appreciation, some amount of exaggeration is made through prior statement which is intended to inspire people to think of themselves a cut above the rest.

Where to avoid: You are required to find out the hidden message beneath the packaging which is intended to serve masked purpose. Especially, when sales person tries to motivate you about taking a decision about you or your family but suppressing the fact that he want to sell you an insurance policy, you should definitely search the motives behind inspiring you to take a decision.

Bias about self [d]

We very often know we also have the judgmental biases like other people have. Still we consider ourselves relatively unbiased and do not compensate sufficiently for our biases. American researchers (Pronin, Lin and Ross) described in their paper, how we are biased to a set of people, and yet they still used that bias in decisions. In their paper control group rated peers and other Americans as having significantly more bias than themselves.

Example: If we undergo an IQ test which shows ourselves as having a lower IQ, we believe that test method is wrong. We tend to find another test which shows us as having a very high IQ, even though the test is less credible.

Usage of bias: The effects of bias can be utilized to motivate people who are under performer due to lack of skill and knowledge - even if they know you are trying to motivate, there will be positive result.

Where to avoid: Realize consciously about your biases. Avoid especially when someone seems to be using your bias blind spot against you for selling a bad proposal.

Bias over perspective

It is very often observed, we compare attributes and achievement of our colleagues, friends in a time long back from present time, where the other person was inferior to us in terms of some particular quality or achievement at that point of time. In case he or she progressed in greater extent than us, it is felt unusual and inappropriate. It is largely because we tend to rate ourselves higher than others even if it tells the different story.

Example: When an individual, working in large organization gets promoted, he compares his position with respect to other colleagues who got promotion, and analyze situation at ten years back where he remained in lower position and he try to find a colleague with identical position in present time but had lesser potential in the past. In case the other person remained lower position say ten year back, his present parallel position seems inappropriate to him.

Usage of bias: The bias can be utilized to motivate people who are presently dissatisfied about their present position and cannot see bright future ahead. Whenever the bias is used against you, try to search out evaluation criteria, whether only time is the essence or performance or any other attribute has got to do anything in it.

Where to avoid: People, who were once friends or classmates, may turn high achiever or under achiever in your time, but should be taken those easy. Find out means they followed resources they have used and your thinking would turn logical.

Bias over supportive alliance

Individuals tend to align in group or another individual if mental support or comfort is received by way of supportive, motivational comments or communications, even if the issue is completely irrational or illogical. The reverse is also true; if anybody receives demoralizing verbal transaction, a resistance is built up within him or her and he or she keeps himself away from that group or individual. Cohesive groups are formed amongst the same opinion holders.

Example: Suppose you are travelling in train with all unknown people around. Someone, say Mr. A initiated a topic of current failure of public transport system, say late running of train or poor service offered by railway. If you comment like this, "In recent time, trains are perfectly running on time, especially since Mr. X has taken the charge of railway minister, no train is observed with more than half an hour late, no train in past three months has been cancelled in northern railway and ever since they have outsourced the cleaning vendors, trains are cleaner than before, every station having more than 10 minutes halt, train compartment are offered to cleaning staff."

Someone else, say Mr. B comments "Whenever I travelled in any train I saw littered toilet. Surely the condition has deteriorated."

Deciding upon the conversation, Mr. A will be aligned to Mr. B even if there is no concrete evidence in his statement but he can find psychological comfort by supporting his opinion. Even though you have presented sufficient evidences supporting to your statement, Mr. A will not get attracted to you, he will refrain to comment on you further.

Usage of bias: Political leaders are prone to exploit this bias of the people by giving populist statements in media. When a large segment of population is pursuing to any specific (may be illogical) demand, political leader earns popularity of that segment by giving supportive statements.

Where to avoid: Whenever you are at the receiving end, try to analyze motive behind such statements. For an HR person, it is essential to see demoralized employees are not aligned to become 'deprived soul mates'. To decide upon a political leader, analyze his past decision and statements - whether it was populist or logical.

Bounded Rationality [g]

Being a rational creature human kind opts rationality in decision making when problem is simple to understand and explainable by logic. Whenever we find the problem complex and unexplainable in the domain of logical understanding, we go for other easier processes. The limit of rationality is imposed by individual on subjective judgment; not only we keep away from logic behind, but also we refrain to devote time or we perceive that it would take more time to derive the decision making in logical processes.

Analysis of complex and harder situation require intense and in-depth thinking, resulting in increase of cognitive load on brain. If it calls for more thinking about the causes behind, thus we leave it to limited choices which reduce the cognitive overload coping to our capabilities. Many of our decisions, as a result are not based on logical thought process. There are many causes of limited rationality few of which are:

F. Limitations of resources for thinking process

G. Mind frame and perceptions.

H. Preoccupation of mind.

I. Prejudices

J. Environmental factors like, peer pressure, family pressure.

K. Cultural background and upbringing.

Example: Someone may choose a model of car which is bought by others and talked about within peer group, even if a better model or make is available in your purchasing capability.

Usage: For selling an object which has many features, a few popular usages can be given to customer to choose easily.

How to avoid: Whenever you are to make decision, assess your capabilities, let it be shared amongst your friends allowing them to offer viewpoints on what seems rational and adequate. Do not be hurried to follow others.

Biased inequality [h]

If we show ourselves rational and equal towards anyone who is under privileged, we correct our bias heavily and try to grab his or her more attention or advantages than others resulting in inequality and bias on reverse side.

Some politicians try to be 'politically correct' being a favourite to underprivileged breaking the rules of equality and fraternity. We found in judiciary for trial of any actual convict, who has committed crime, the lawyer of convict try to overemphasize on inadmissibility of any law, such as witness is brought without any prior permission of court etc. Although statement of witness can fairly resolve the case against convict, defending lawyer tries to prove illegitimacy of hearing of witness. Here the rationale goes against the rulebook.

Example: When we try to treat womenfolk as an equal partner in work life, we try to give extra advantage than male counterpart. Or in case we see a women standing in bus, train people offer seat, or any public service, queue for women is separate, which give them extra advantage results in treatment more than equal or less than equal.

How to avoid: In case you feel that you may show bias or overcompensate in the opposite direction, consider yourself somebody else, who can point out the bias on reverse side.

Causality based Self Determination

Every person has 'perceived locus of causality' or PLOC with a limit beyond which they need external forces from outside for initiating any action including decision making. PLOC can be internal which is linked to intrinsic or self motivation and external PLOC which is linked to external or extrinsic motivation. With an internal PLOC a person feels self motivated to become the initiator and sustains their actions. They make their behaviour as evolving out of their own choices based on their perception, values, and interests while persons with an external PLOC see their behaviour controlled by some external forces like influential person, demanding situation etc.

Example: A person with low internal high external PLOC always complains about his life as he experiences controlling his life by others or external force like working life and low earning. On the contrary, a person with high internal PLOC controls his own life and feels himself responsible for each and every act.

Usage: In order to motivate people try to find out whether they have stronger internal or external locus and act accordingly to persuade.

How to avoid: For assessment of self and regulation, it is necessary to understand your own locus of control. Self motivation with a link to cause and effect improves internal PLOC.

Sustenance Criterion

Sometimes our short term desires do not bring about long term good; whatever we desire is obviously not good for us even if it results in short term pleasure. Spicy and rich food, sedentary lifestyle, avoidance of physical exercise may give you instant comfort but will prove to be harmful in the long run.

Similar way, if a doctor suggests you to physical exercise daily, then you may require to have enough self-discipline to implement and sustaining the same.

It is noted that implementation and sustenance of difficult task requires self regulation. It is not always the difficulty of the task that stopping us for sustenance, sometime we evaluate small additional effort multiplied by length of term trading off long term benefit. Just as hyperbolic discounting, we ignore the long term benefit.

The nature has designed sustenance of effort and good practice for choosing the long term benefit over short term good (long term harm in disguise) to be left at will of species in survival race. It is to ensure that best chooser exists in long run and on the other hand worse chooser is supposed to succumb to eventualities.

Example: If a person quit alcoholism or any other die hard habits, it is very likely it will relapse after sometime if self regulation is not adopted in strict terms.

Usage: Exercising self regulation requires clear objectives emphasizing on how someone can get benefitted following a self regulation path. If benefit is likely to be obtained in long run, highlight other small short term benefit to appease self and others on similar path.

How to avoid: Where something is very difficult to achieve or avoid, go step by step. If sustenance is achieved in first step then go for next level of difficulty.

Comparative satisfaction Bias

Individuals compare their peers, friends, colleagues, classmates or amongst similar group, about their progress, achievement, hurdles, setbacks and other attributes to get the satisfaction. If anyone finds himself in a better position within comparison group, he gets satisfaction, no matter what is the extent of it. Similarly, anyone who is supposed to be happy after getting what he wanted may feel dissatisfied if he finds that it has been attained by someone else who he considers him inferior to his comparison group.

Example: Employees in a large organization, tend to get dissatisfied if they did not get upgradation in time, especially when they find other colleagues got it by that time. In case, he finds himself incomparable in same organization, he may also compare himself with classmates in other organization just to decide whether he should be satisfied or dissatisfied.

Usage: This bias can be utilized for motivating people to give their best potential among his or her group. Even if everyone knows in competitive environment, less no of participants get satisfaction, person with reasonable quantum of optimism tries to reach top.

Where to avoid: Getting satisfaction over other people's failure or setback is the worst case of this bias. Harming self by seeing others progress is also a similar blunder, one can commit. In order to avoid this, Compare and compete only with self, you will find yourself definitely in a better position.

Prejudice over prejudice

Getting biased over avoiding prejudice is termed as prejudice over prejudice. It may appear like biased inequality but differs from it in way that prejudice over prejudice is a conscious and biased attempt to show that the action is devoid of prejudice, whereas, biased inequality is unconscious or subconscious attempt favouring extra justice to under-privileged. The idea of "Justice appearing to have done" or "not getting prejudiced" involves conscious attempt to avoid bias, however being conscious about not appearing biased, something extra effort is done in such a manner that it is very often resulted in reverse prejudice.

Example: In most of the road accident cases where a two wheeler and four wheeler are involved, four wheelers are fined more as a cause of accident; in such cases prejudice being prevalent on reverse side just to make justice appear to have done. In court proceedings on criminal cases, the convict gets more time to produce defence evidence, which is a type of prejudice over prejudice. Another type of prejudice may occur, while taking an action which may be considered by others, having a prejudice to be correlated with; however in true sense there is no physical prejudice existed. If you do not take action in such cases, you are actually prejudiced over prejudice. However, if you take action, it may not appear that you are free of prejudice. Suppose, a multi religion nation decide to ban religious activities in public places, it may appear that that nation is not secular based on the religion of majority of population. However, if the nation rolls back the decision, it supports prejudice over prejudice.

Usage: Taking stock of the situation and getting prejudiced over prejudice is not definitely a rational decision. However, where large cross section of people or their feelings are getting affected, it is practical to go for "appeared truth" rather than "real truth".

How to avoid: The bias can be avoided at ease when you go by logic and prevalent laid down principle.

Known devil Liking

If repeated exposure is given as a stimulus, people will tend to like it for familiarity, which breeds liking rather than disapproval. There are many examples in day to day life where everyone tends to like an object or environment after getting used to it. Starting from choosing a career, earning, settling in a location, fixing life partner all get familiar with the passage of time and being liked more than the initial encounter. Just like students miss their school life even if the schooling was substandard, a prisoner misses jail, even if the experience was frightful.

Similarly we sometimes opt for the familiar one out of many unfamiliar choices as "Known devil is preferable than unknown angel".

For launching a new commercial product, repeated advertising of the same creates liking and buyer is initiated to purchase.

It is also known that over exposure or repetition can cause harm to liking. After a certain number of exposures cycle, people will not only ignore but also tends to hate it. In case it crosses the tolerable limit, it causes irritation as felt while seeing over repeated ad in TV. Negative effect is resulted from mind change for harming the privacy or peace and mind is set for taking revenge. That is why ads of same product get changes time to time but having the same messages.

Usage: In order to convince a customer for a car to sell, free test drive is offered to him so as to get him familiarized which may be converted to liking of the model.

How to avoid: Just focus on your objectives. Whenever you are fallen prey to it, have a conscious thought of whether you liked it for familiarity.

Camouflaged counter bias

Whenever counter bias is created for any benefit of larger mass protecting the prevailing law, it requires to be camouflaged, since it is vulnerable to be countered by opposition.

Counter bias is also created for bad intentions. Many fraudulent money laundering racketeers create counter bias highlighting their credential by disbursing excellent return on short term investment to limited initial subscribers. Later on when their credibility is established they deceive the large masses who later on fall prey to their scheme.

Usage: So as to emphasize no-bias for taking any decision to turn down on proposer's face, he may be allowed to initiate which can be ruled out later on by a committee.

How to avoid: Whenever you are at the receiving end, just convince everyone to follow your suit.

Case Study

Rajat Kumar Gupta, a Mechanical Engineering graduate from IIT Delhi eventually became Indian-American businessman philanthropist who was serving a two-year jail term in US federal prison for the charge of insider trading. He was the first Indian born Chief Executive of management consultancy firm McKinsey & Company and also being a board member of corporations including Goldman Sachs, Procter and Gamble and American Airlines. Rajat Kumar Gupta has also illustrated philanthropic, charitable and volunteered efforts on the areas of education, global health; cofounded Indian School of Business, Scandent solutions, New silk Route etc. He has been attached to several universities and other non-profit organizations, serving as chairman and member of several boards and councils and rose to rare heights in corporate America and became the poster boy of the Indian-American success story.

He was convicted in June 2012 on insider trading charges of four criminal felony counts of conspiracy and securities fraud. On trial the Manhattan Federal court sentenced him in October 2012 for two years in prison and huge monetary fine.

The case of Mr. Rajat Gupta may be defined in "moral credential bias" where his unquestionable reputation has led to creating a supporting environment which turned him to lose his age old principle.

CHAPTER-13

Optimal well being and life satisfaction

"The part can never be well unless the whole is well" -
Plato

"In minds crammed with thoughts, organs clogged with toxins, and bodies stiffened with neglect, there is just no space for anything else" -**Alison Rose Levy**

"Health is a state of complete physical, mental and social well-being, and not merely the absence of disease or infirmity" -**World Health Organization**

Very often we casually estimate our state of well being with available conventional yard stick; keeping pace with the time we move ahead, comparing parameters suitable to others and not being understood real essence of well being. Mostly we refer physical healthiness as a true meaning of it. However, well being constitutes peace of our body, mind and existence in the society and relationship. Since well being is relative, sometimes each constituent impacts others, some are achieved forgoing others and requires optimization of the same. Let us find out what optimal well being is.

Optimal well being is keeping balance among all aspects of well being maximizing the positive energy most of the time. You have to choose the right path rationally so as to keep positive energy through maximizing emotional motive force. Right blend of rational and emotional impetus is dependent more on normative or heuristic approach rather than logical manner as it is personalized for every individual. How much rationality can be imposed is mostly governed entirely by view point of individual.

Being well and healthy is as much important as achieving a goal in life time. Health is manifestation of state of mind and body emphasizing sound physical and emotional well being.

Norman B. Anderson, an American Psychologist emphasizes six dimensions of health:

Biological well-being: your tangible structure and the five senses which enable you to touch, see, hear, smell and taste the world around you

Psychological and behavioural well-being: your range of emotions from fear and anger to love and joy

Environmental and social well-being: your social status

Economic well-being: Your financial capabilities

Existential, religious, spiritual well-being: Understanding self actualization and meaningfulness

Emotional well-being: Psychological, emotional and behavioural wellness.

However, for the sake of practical understanding, we may categorize all categories of well beings into four major groups:

Biological or physical well-being

Emotional well-being:

Economic well-being

Social well being

Finding Optimal Limits of well being

The quest for well being may start with identification of key areas to be monitored. For identification of key area, objectives shall be benchmarked first so as to define "where and why we would like to go". In any form of well being, evaluate whether we should keep along the present state of being or to improve to certain level. Check whether, our economic status, social need, physical health, mental and psychological statuses are perfectly matching to our satisfaction.

Optimal limits are not meant to be set but to be understood in process of progress. The trend of progress gives you an impression about how much time is required for achievement of what. Being conscious about the limits helps maintain inertia level up to the brim whenever you are on the go. Too much extension of limits beyond capabilities saps energy and demoralizes you to be drop-out.

Setting up priorities

Set up priorities among all aspects of well beings to achieve one after another or some at a time. Most of the objectives can run in parallel or in compliment to each other. Keeping on progressing on good physical well being, helps push you extra bit to achieve economic well being. Improvement of economic status attracts social needs which can be fulfilled utilizing time management. By socializing you will get positive energy by way of inspiration and encouragement to give more impetus to your hard work.

Finding right strategies towards objectives

It is very essential to know right strategies to be fruitful meeting objectives. Choosing strategies under uncertainty is difficult but can be made simpler by way of probabilistic approach for choosing more rationally. Sometimes, the situation cannot generate sufficient data to fit this approach. Heuristic approach can be helpful in few cases, if necessary, where reversal is viable. There are many tools like case studies, past experiences, success stories, upgradation of knowledge through experts, peers on relevant field, which have potential to guide you finding strategies. Whatever strategies are adopted it has to be monitored after implementation, requires fine tune or even substantial changes.

Implementation of strategies

One of the most difficult parts in path of achievement lies in implementation. Since all natural changes require extra energy to break the inertia, implementation does not defy the law of nature. Mental inertia plays the major role in putting back the implementation in cold box. Rational understanding of mental barrier and conscious action is required for breaking all barriers to implement any strategy. And your job is half done with a good start.

Sustenance

The essence of success is to make it habitual by way of sustenance. Keep going with broadened mind set to achieve more as there is no static state, which has ever survived for long. The sustenance means to progress further and to achieve more and to get it better; then the present situation will pass through dynamic changes resulting in survival against bites of time.

Ingredients of Life satisfaction

Satisfaction and happiness is entirely subjective and relative. What life satisfaction is ought to be, differs in person-to-person approach based on their perception about of life, present standpoint and comparative to environs they live in. Life satisfaction and striving for it drives individual to get him ahead or plays vital role in balancing act between choosing different lifestyle. We tend to measure life satisfaction in three different ways: through pleasure (hedonism), through engagement, and through meaningfulness and our well being is dependent on mixture of these ingredients.

An individual if found simultaneously low on all three orientations, is reported to have low life satisfaction and reverse. At the both extremes there lie full life and empty life.

Wikipedia defines life satisfaction as:

Life satisfaction is the way a person perceives how his or her life has been and how they feel about where it is going in the future. It is a measure of well-being and may be assessed in terms of mood, satisfaction with relations with others and with achieved goals, self-concepts, and self-perceived ability to cope with daily life. It is having a favourable attitude of one's life as a whole rather than their current feelings. Life satisfaction has been measured in relation to economic standing, amount of education, experiences, and the people's residence as well as many other topics.

Going back to ancient times, revealed that first formulated doctrine of life satisfaction evolved around hedonism which was focused to maximize pleasure and minimize pain. It was introduced by Aristuppus circa 400BCE who emphasized immediate sensory gratification to attain pleasure. It was further moderated by Epicurus (342–270 BCE) through ethical hedonism, which restrained people by fundamental moral obligation towards maximizing experience of pleasure. However later on next generation Christian philosophers denounced hedonism as it was falling inconsistent with the goal of avoiding sin. In eighteenth century Jeremy Bentham founded utilitarianism using doctrine of hedonism. Hedonism is still alive in various form of formulation of philosophy not only in western world but in every part of globe which drives people for achieving happiness without pain.

In distinct contrast to hedonism there was another tradition evolved in circa 350BCE through Aristotle's notion of eudemonia which means "being true to one's inner self". According to this view, true happiness involve identifying, maturing and following one's virtues if life. In modern era

Maslow introduced various needs of the individuals encountered throughout his life and laid concept of self actualization. Based upon eudemonic concepts later philosophers develop what is best within them and then use these skills and talents in the service of society at large. In the modern world, the pursuit of a meaningful life is widely endorsed to achieve ''be everything you are capable make a world of difference.''

The pursuit of life as engagement has been elaborated by Csikszentmihalyi and Seligman who emphasized life is supported by flow of activities. The consciousness about self is forgotten in performing activities utilizing precious time that runs so quickly. The sense of self is never felt as individual is engrossed always in finding challenging task to defeat time and individual is completely lost within to extract his best ability to finish the task.

Although well being and life satisfaction is somewhat subjective and each individual's perception is a blend of three orientations as stated above, satisfaction as such can be measurable when putting it on a scale which is built up from the subjective notion.

Modern behavioural scientist formulated life satisfaction quantified it in the form of measuring scale with assumed yard stick. One of such methods is devised by *Diener, E., Emmons, R. A., Larsen, R. J., & Griffin, S. (1985) elaborated as under:*

Scale: The scale is devised on basic Instructions of five statements that you may agree or disagree with.

Using the 1 - 7 scale below, individual's agreement with each statement by choosing the appropriate number corresponding to it.

7.Strongly agree

6.Agree

5.Slightly agree

4.Neither agree nor disagree

3.Slightly disagree

2.Disagree

1. Strongly disagree

Statement about satisfaction

Statement	Score
In most ways my life is close to my ideal	5
The conditions of my life are excellent	5
I am satisfied with my life	5
So far I have gotten the important things I want in life	5
If I could live my life over, I would change almost nothing	1
Total	21

Scoring: Though scoring should be kept continuous (sum up scores on each item), here are some cut-offs to be used as benchmarks.

31 - 35 Extremely satisfied

26 - 30 Satisfied

21 - 25 Slightly satisfied

20 - Neutral

15 - 19 Slightly dissatisfied

10 - 14 Dissatisfied

5 - 9 Extremely dissatisfied

Similar type of evaluation can also be developed by anybody on their own keeping in view the necessity of their short term and long term desire. But all such evaluation method employs comparison only with self desire, but relinquishes comparison of achievement with respect to what others have accomplished. It is always to be remembered sense of having accomplished is subjective as there is no such case of ultimate achievement per se. Thus emphasizing comparison with self in terms of what criteria you considered most to be satisfied shall be the fruitful idea to take it as yardstick to measure whether you have achieved now or not. It is utilized to decide even for achievement in future.

The catch: Satisfaction does not understand numbers, your feeling will always override calculation and quantification.

Physical and emotional Wellness: Holistic Approach

Physical wellness is having ingredients of key health parameters like more energy, greater enthusiasm and love towards life, greater sense of joy and life satisfaction. Wellness is emerged and felt from within but manifests in outward look which is distinct and can also be seen and felt by others.

In recent times more numbers of people are becoming aware to the true meaning of balanced health, comprising of physical, mental, emotional health, which form the foundation of a happy, satisfied and fulfilled life.

The building blocks, in which holistic approach to health is built upon, is in fact the idea of wholesome healthiness having unity of goodness, natural flow of life, the harmonious and right balance of the physical, mental, and psychological aspects of wellness.

Within this domain of perfect wholeness, life may also often stuck up with daily chores and distractions of life, but uniqueness of our true selves remains within intact which guides us to right direct direction. We may very often meet challenging situations creating temporary 'imbalance', but our wholeness eventually wins and heals the imperfection in short time.

A complete wellness comprises of

• Right balance of physical, emotional, mental, and spiritual health

• Good social environment earning you respectful, cooperative relationships with your family, friends, and relatives.

Taxonomy of wellness characteristics

Character	Purely Optimistic	Optimized optimist	Optimized pessimist	Purely pessimist
Health Strategy	Avoid preventive checks	Preventive lifestyle with no checks	Preventive checks from young age	Preventive checks and lifestyle
Work out regime	No interest, hedonic lifestyle	Moderate Work out without no preventive care	Moderate workout with preventive care	No interest, away from life
Relation-ship	open	independent	Counselling	possessive
Values	Idealistic	Easy-believer	Practical	Cynic
Ethical character	True	Trustworthy	Dependable	Dishonest

Visualizing mind-body interaction

Mind-body interaction cannot be well understood unless we visualize chemical reactions which are taking place inside the body every moment. What causes pain, what makes us laugh, what can cause excitement, how can we remain in blissful pleasure even if we undergo severe physical discomfort have been subject of research for practitioner of modern medical science and social psychology. Modern medical science has discovered various brain chemicals which affects our mood and reaction of our body.

It is now proven that human brain releases chemicals called endorphins in the blood to produce a feeling of well being in the event of pain, excitement, euphoria, danger, exercise, love, sexual activity and even consumption of spicy food. The word endorphin consists of two words 'endogenous' which means 'having internal cause or origin' and 'morphine' which is a pain inhibiting chemicals. Combined meaning of endorphins is 'morphine-like substance originating from within the body' A better understanding of how these positive brain chemicals can be enhanced would help transform your lifestyle towards physical and mental wellness.

Endorphins are known as neurotransmitters which cause to transmit electrical signals within the nervous system. Beta-endorphin is released by pituitary gland in brain which mixes into blood from hypothalamic neurons in brain and spinal cord. Stress and pain are the two most common factors leading to the release of endorphins.

Beta-endorphin has the highest affinity for the opioid receptor, which are the main receptor through which morphine acts and these receptors are pre-synaptic, and inhibit neurotransmitter release. Through that mechanism, they inhibit the release of the inhibitory neurotransmitter GABA (Gamma Amino-butyric acid), and cause more dopamine to be released.

In addition to feeling of reduced pain, secretion of endorphins manifests in feelings of euphoria, enhancement of the immune system response, modulation of appetite, release of sex hormones. With high endorphin levels, we feel less pain and fewer negative effects of stress.

There are several ways to activate releasing high endorphin in human body which may include drugs also. However, natural and habitual ways which preferred over drug therapy.

Few Pointers on lifestyle changes impacting emotional well being

In order to maintain increased level of endorphin which in turn helps maintain your emotional wellness the following mental habits may be adopted:

Put your mind on the go: Pseudo-sense of alertness for keeps your mind running for next higher achievement, puts your mind and body always on the go and makes senses blind to negative reactions. Staying on positive emotion maintains high level of endorphins.

Meditation and breathing exercises: Deep breathing exercises causes absorption of more oxygen results in higher O2 level in blood by activating idle portion of the lungs. In course of meditation, CO2 and other toxins also get released from tissues and get it cleansed from stress chemicals. Meditation help dissociating from stresses of active mind and help un-focusing self towards de-stressing. Relaxation from meditation gets you positive feeling and release of endorphins.

Smile and laugh: Smiling releases endorphins which make you feel good. It is helpful watching comedy show and interacting people with jovial mood so that pleasant feeling is evoked and pleasure is felt deep within heart. Although smile and laugh are the reactions of happiness, but being reversible in nature, it helps create and feel pleasure out of it.

Follow the guts: There is something to do with gut feeling. It is now proven that your eating habits, choices of tastes etc. are desires of the bacterium in your gut. Even intoxication by tobacco, alcohols is also controlled by those organisms. Therefore beware of indulging in any habits which could develop a certain type of bacterium which would compel you to keep that habit.

Physical work out: It is well established that endorphin is raised when you are done with vigorous exercise and you feel good all over. Your will even feel stronger for few hours after you are done with work out.

Be Happy: Body and mind is having synergic relationship. If you feel happier your body will get healthier and vice versa. Feeling of happiness raises endorphin in body. Feel happier with all your current achievement. Unfocus the matters whatever you would have not got due to lack of your personal reasons.

Follow good eating habits: Eat just, avoid overeating. Adding just one piece of dark chocolate a day will make you happier. Add spice to your food up to tolerable limit.

Whenever you eat chilli or pepper your body will stimulate to secrete endorphin more.

Add entertainment to your life! Relish, entertain yourself out of anything, listen to your favourite tune and relax from mundane daily life. Music is an effective stress reliever to let you live in your present time and capable of enhancing your endorphin level.

Socialize: Interact with people, socialize with whoever you know and especially the people you have come across for the first time and your endorphins will be released by your body. Healthy and positive interaction is fruitful exercise for well being.

Getaway with near and dear one: Spending vacation with near and dear one can not only get your stress relieved but have the ability to rediscover yourself and your relationship which is considered one of the most effective enhancer of endorphin.

Criteria: There is way to limit conventional medicines
Nature has designed our physiological system with self healing properties to fight with microorganism causing disease, maintains blood chemicals by purifying systems through kidney, sweat gland, lungs etc. Although in entire lifetime a man may not fall sick, still the body will undergo degeneration process where bone, immunity, metabolism, nervous system, endocrine glands, get affected with the passage of time. The degeneration is obvious but can be significantly slowed down if we maintain good habits paying heed to our system adopting

following natural processes for slowing down the degeneration:

Control contaminants: Because of our unhealthy eating habits irreversible contamination takes place in blood vessel, and other organ like lever, kidney, pancreas etc. Body is to adopt our overdrive for food intake trading off the life of corresponding organ. It is a fact that contaminant's main entry is our mouth and if we control our food, we are sure to make the process slower and get rid of diseases. Consult nutritionist to opt food according to your age. Maintain immunity by healthy food intake enriched with vitamins and minerals. If the foods are insufficient, take supplement. Doctor's and nutritionist's advice may be fruitful to avoid contacting disease and maintaining immunity.

Control degeneration: Maintain the control over food intake, timing, physical activity and easy enhancer of metabolism. Few simple enhancers like walking have great impact on your metabolism.
Slow down degeneration by keeping active body and mind. The degeneration of body and its sub systems can be controlled by food. The mind degeneration can be controlled by knowledge. Reading books, social activities have positive effect on this. Even some of the nervous degenerative disease can be controlled by keeping brain active. It is proven that mind-body coordination plays greater role to control degeneration. If you continue to think young, you obviously get your system age slower. In numerous experiments, it is noted that even if you think or

visualize without doing things, you get part of desired outcome which is expected in doing things. However, opposing mind-body action nullifies each other, just like if you over eat and think it is good for health, you may not get advantage.

Preventive checks: we all know prevention is always better than cure, but we are reluctant to check or monitor our health parameter as we grow old or even try to remain in self satisfying false belief that we would be immune to all such criticalities. Several degenerative diseases set in as we simply do not know where it began and get unpleasant surprise when it turns out be irreversible and incurable. Physical parameters like body weight, blood pressure, blood parameters including functional test for organs and other preventive checks as per advice of doctor obviously help reducing chances of critical ailments.

Psychological/Emotional Wellness
Most of us agree that our sense of positive outcome comes from experiences of life events and state of our mental framework. Going with Adams, Bezner, and Steinhardt, 1997; Leafgren, 1990). Hettler (1980), Emotional wellness can be defined as conscious control of feelings and emotional reactions, sense of the self, conflict scenario, managing stressful circumstances and emergencies and the fulfilling relationships with others.
Emotional wellness encompasses inquisitiveness and query to life, experimenting and experiencing satisfaction creating positive expectations of the future.
We may well agree that life satisfaction is very much subjective as it mostly depends on perceiving happiness

which is purely a subjective matter. Even it is seen that personality of individual influence perception of happiness and satisfaction.

According to Harrington and Loffredo (2001) people who are more self-conscious and introverted scoring lower levels of life satisfaction than extroverts. However, the dimensions of extroversion produce varying results. As per Diener and colleagues (1999) extroverts are more comfortable in social situations. In other psychological aspects like managing stressful situations and emergencies, they may not be as uncomfortable as introverts.

Emotional well being involves the fulfilment of basic psychological needs: independence, competence, and intrinsic motivation, integrity and achievement of life satisfaction.

Hales (2005) includes trust, self-esteem, self acceptance, self-confidence, self-control, and the ability to bounce back from setbacks and failures as important wellness attributes.

Emotional wellness calls for up-keep of mental status by indulging in exploratory thoughts or feelings, identifying mistakes in day to day life and its rectification, maintaining relationship with warmth and positivism.

Economic well being

The modern times cannot deny the importance of economic well being of individual which help maintain sustenance of present and shapes the future. Obviously the balance between present and future depends on optimization spending and making resources for future. The optimal balance between earning money and investing for the future not only lead to respectable life but can create wealth for the future. Irrespective of what professions you are in, economic well being will follow few broad principles:

Start early: Even if you are young start investing early. Shaping the future becomes easy and attaining wealth predominantly depends on how early you have started investing.

Capitalize on time: Opportunity and right strategy touch everyone. Never miss to capitalize on time as procrastination and indecisiveness lead to despair. The cost of not taking a decision is always much more than decision not yielding result.

Define financial hits: There must be major financial hits in everyone's life. Prior awareness of such hits makes you prepare for the same and help you make the road map for achieving.

Just Invest not to save: Differentiate saving from investment. Save for short run future, and remember, saving for the long term will be eaten away by inflation. Invest for the long term gain gaining edge over inflation and devaluation.

Insure rationally: Insurance for life, good health and protecting other assets are pessimistic approach to ensure least impact from eventualities. Insure rationally to keep balance between protecting present in future and shaping the future as per present visualization.

Uncertainty in economic well being

Our economic cycle changes periodically and most of the people experience the gloom and boom. Over the last 50 years, there have been 7-8 bear markets and equal nos .bull markets. People turn conservative and are taking low risk during recession period. However optimistic view towards economic changes always pays. If we keep our positive approach in bear markets, it can turn to bull more quickly. Some of the market leaders are adopting recession defying strategies to take care and boost up mass psychology during difficult period. We must remember high will surely follow the low; the more we expect the sooner it will emerge.

Social Wellness

Individuals are connected to others for fulfilling mental, psychological and social needs. Social Wellness refers to his or her interaction with people around and how well he or she is recognized by others. Having good communications skills, having meaningful relationships with near and dear, friends, colleagues and others, and society at large are the attributes of social well being.

Social wellness may constitute the following objectives:

- Contributing positively towards society to satisfy self
- Creating harmony and sense of belongingness with others

• Resolving conflicts and getting back to state of psychological normalcy.

Have we achieved social wellness? What are factors that attribute social wellness? The following question may be asked to ourselves to know where we are in path of social wellness:

• Do I spent time with family and friends and are they satisfied with my skill of work life balance?

• Am I enjoying spending with others and feel relationship rewarding?

• Do I cross the boundary when I meet unknown people and they greet me in future?

• Do I value social needs of fellow colleagues and other who are surrounding me in work life?

If we get satisfactory answer to all of the above we are just right on the path; if not obviously we have to take action.

Hedonic treadmill

In 1971 Brickman P. and Campbell D. first coined the term in their paper "Hedonic Relativism and Planning the Good Society". In late 1990s, the concept was further modified by Michael Eysenck, a British psychologist, to become the current "hedonic treadmill theory"

Positive emotions are short lived in human mind, as attaining such happiness would create craving for another. Feeling of deprivation until the next is achieved fades the happiness and the positive emotions gradually diminish. Therefore everyone runs after another goal to get the mirage of happiness. Thus positive emotions lead to the theory of the hedonic treadmill where an individual tries to find new ways to experience new positivity because their old techniques have become ineffective.

The Broaden-and-Build theory addresses this issue to some extent by putting the argument that life satisfaction is achieved through path with positive emotions makes person to build resources to improve life satisfaction for extended periods of time. This process is said to be much more effective to attain life satisfaction than by the path leading to life satisfaction straight from positive emotions due to the hedonic treadmill effect.. A study on these emotions was done over a nine-week period by Fredrickson, Cohn, Coffey, Peck, and Finkel. The period of time allowed them to see that these positive emotions were not developed quickly. The slow development of such state provided evidence that the positive effects built resources that allowed for more positive experience in the future.

Life satisfaction is not only known to be pivotal around individuals' attainment of goal but it has been influenced by the desire for knowledge of new things, where anyone can find connectivity to society, nature and supreme power. Among the positive emotions, inquisitiveness is thus most important which helps explore new things leading to create repertoire of all positive effects required for life satisfaction.

CHAPTER-14

Limiting criteria

"The ability to discipline yourself to delay gratification in the short term in order to enjoy greater rewards in the long term is the indispensable pre-requisite for success" **Brian *Tracy***

"If A is a success in life, then A = x + y + z. Work is x; y is play; and z is keeping your mouth shut"—**Albert Einstein**

Adage goes like this: everything on earth has certain limit to get the desired benefit out of it. Beyond certain dose, any medicine turns out to be harmful to body, below certain limit, poison may find usage as medicine, excess ambition turns to be greediness, and excess honesty invites opportunists to set the stage for evil to overpower. Even excess positivism creates harmful positive fantasy. Limit applies to our universe too; beyond certain mass, a star collapses to become black hole, below such limit it turns to white giant.

There is no such rule that governs all real phenomena; there is no axiom which cannot be refuted by at least one experiment. Here are some criteria cited below which will help understand putting the limits whenever it calls for.

Criteria: Limit positive fantasy

While visualization remaining an important tool for achievement, it alone falls short to get you at the door of success, it necessarily requires moving ahead with aggression with time bound action which fetches elusive success. Positive visualization has to be within its effective rational limits; it must not cross to territory to reach domain of positive fantasy.

Psychologists Heather Barry Kappes and Gabriele Oettingen recently published "Positive Fantasies About Idealized Futures Sap Energy" in the Journal of Experimental Social Psychology. Their conclusion is "the more you visualize having attained a cherished goal, the less likely you are to achieve".

If you create a positive fantasy before attaining a goal you may be able to taste the benefit from your created daydream and without any effort and hard work. Whenever you come back to reality, you realize there is a lot of home work to perform which necessitate putting your time and energy.

Then, should we avoid the positive fantasy?

The answer is "NO". The positive remains positive when blended with positive action. Painless fantasy is not real, if you perceive your positive fantasy as a painless action it has no longer contain a positive effect. Painless fancy can be tolerable up to that limit whenever you would like to elevate your mood for relaxation for a short time. Do not cross the boundary to reach complacency where you energy level may go down to below threshold to maintain inertia.

The catch: Limit your positive visualization up to setting goal instead. Follow rational visualization thereafter.

Criteria: Limit goal with sensibility

You might be aware of the popular folklore of one greedy man. One day he goes to landlord and says 'Please give me some land for my livelihood'. He replied "Take all the land that you can cover in a day by riding your horse but subject to condition that you have to start from here and return here by sunset". The greedy man goes on riding very far not realizing how far he should go so that I would be able to return by sunset. One should set goal for themselves which is sensible and achievable. Keep in mind achieving goal is optional but enjoying achievement without endangering everything else for that matter is mandatory. Be optimal in setting goal based upon realistic estimate of future outcomes.

There are certain mixes of emotional and physical action which result in optimized output. Mix them with proper ingredients and avoid the game spoilers. The thumb rules may be as under:

Action+viualization+zeal= Success

Action+visualization-zeal=underachievement, delayed success.

Inaction+visualization-zeal=Day dreaming

Inaction+visualization+zeal=Stray Effort leading to failure or nonstarter

Action-visualization+zeal=Too many hurdles in path of success

Action-visualization-zeal=Lost motivation due to early failure

Criteria: Some of Positive emotions are negative in disguise

Beware of these positive emotions as they have the potential to make you complacent keeping you choose comfort zone by reducing energy to chase success. Unless you change the perception of satisfaction, happiness, these positive emotions will prove to be counterproductive.

• Satisfaction

• Happiness

• Contentment

The catch: Delay the gratification to achieve more

Criteria: Change your perception of happiness, get satisfied to work more.

It is contrary to general belief but true that happiness can evolve from any simple thing, satisfaction does not need comfort. Since childhood, we have been changing the object of desire; at time we felt happy when we got a plastic toy car, then raised level of our happiness when we learnt to ride bicycle and now we forget to be happy even after owning a car or house. The question is, have we changed ourselves as we grew older or the definition of happiness got changed within us? When we see people around we chase elusive happiness to show we are happier than others. Therefore our feeling of happiness is not exactly revolving around achieving object of desire but on acquiring more than others. Our benchmark of fullness is limitless therefore it does need the skill of upbringing the self and you can satisfy your inner self without help of any object of desire. If we change our mode of feeling happy towards giving more to society, we will certainly enjoy our work and get satisfaction even after hard work.

Criteria: Few Negative emotions are useful for getting desired energy level for success

We are aware that anger is the most seductive of all emotions as having the largest amount of energy which is mostly uncontrollable. The source of energy if converted to utilize in the passion you will get amazing result. To overcome the intermittent setbacks on your way to success requires avenging mode. Convert the energy of rage resulting out of failure to pull you back from domain of despair. Get going with the working energy derived from aggression.

Criteria: The probability of turning a negative into positive outcome is conditional on subject

Sometimes, it is very difficult to identify the outcome. Whereas apparent outcome may seem negative, it has potential to be positive in future. You may also require

Change in the game plan which requires individual drive and perseverance and attitude that never accept "NO".

Criteria: Happiness lies in the present time

We tend to see happiness conditional on several desires and attainment of those, thus relishing the success become elusive as we tend achieve more to satisfy self. We value for what is yet to achieve rather than what we have achieved so far. Our celebration for present success is thus getting postponed in expectation of more as we enjoy ride over hedonic treadmill. Work for getting satisfaction than to win happiness. Celebrate every milestone so that your entire journey becomes pleasant.

The catch: Optimize greed with gratification to control momentum as well as overcoming boredom.

Criteria: Your health is your choice, when you draw limit to living

Many of us think that our health is fully dependent on quality of health care we receive and how much we can spend on it. As a result we try to earn as much as we can and save for the future even at the cost of health, and when our lives head towards bad health the entire saving is diminished to recover or retain health. You may be amazed, to preserve good health choosing the healthy lifestyle, creating the right fitness regime, you can maintain both, your tangible wealth and your intangible wealth called health.

Your choices begin from every short step you take every day on your own behalf. You decide to form habits, acquire and quit good, bad and evil leading to either wellness or decay until you realize it affected your health.

At the beginning if your choice is good, it will earn you wellness and if it is bad it takes you to despair.

It is obvious that single lifetime offers us only one golden opportunity to make irreversible and unrepeatable journey of life and our state of well being on this voyage; very often indicates difference between the progress we made to become and what we meant to become. Sometimes we experience imbalance of wellness and our harmony is challenged and we find opportunities to reassuring the balance. Every action we made, manifests in a certain outcome, thus our choice is important to lead ourselves in the right path.

The catch: Your progress should always remind you that health is an asset.

Criteria: It is better not to get indulged as to transform later is more difficult

At certain stage, it may require bringing about change of state, which is phenomenal or paradigm shift as seemed may be. Every transformation is prone to die or reversal to original state is obvious unless strategic steps are followed. Say for example, someone who is addicted in certain die hard habits may experience these stages to quit or to transform into new rehabilitated life or he may quit the strategy itself not finding out the steps for further progress.

When someone is completely unaware of the side effects or ignores even after knowing it but sees the short term positive side of indulgence of the newly acquired habits the addiction sets in. He or she may try to find companion in indulgence to the habit until it forms to be full blown pathological addict. Even if by some time the addict has known a few things about side effects but ignores with justification with the statistics, that many of addicts get along with this lifelong and nothing could happen to them even if other may be affected.

Criteria: Ethical limit is subjective

Any individual may follow ethics on the basis of value system built within oneself through upbringing. Being human he cannot walk over the tight rope of rationality. On the path of fulfilling one's desires, he may become selfish and deviate ways at his convenience. As a result, ethical acceptable limits are crossed by individuals considering his obstacles and advantages. Moral boundaries such as fairness, integrity are to prevent us from falling apart from domain of conscience. However, life is complex and complicated and bounded by the many forces to combat, at the same time we have the freedom of choice and natural inclination to cross the boundaries. In the process of making life more comfortable we try to push the ethical boundaries to set the new limits of right and wrong.

Good ethics is the balancing work between desire for fulfilling wishes and available choice in our life. The stronger the feeling to fulfil the desire by means which considered unfair the more we get ourselves off from the ethical path.

Criteria: Limit of Determinism

In this real world, occurrence of any event is not truly deterministic nor does it preclude usage of probability in finding chances of happening an event. If we define the events with activities of elementary particles constituting physical bodies, then events are the effects of location and velocities of these particles. We are already aware that going with the knowledge of physics, the material determinism is solely dependable on location and velocities of each every particle, which cannot be presumed with certainty; and this uncertainty leads to viewpoints that the world cannot be truly deterministic. Thus the knowledge can never be enough to ascertain eventualities in the future in accordance with nature of past event with precise accuracy. The events are not truly random either so much as to probability can be applied to ensure its correct likelihood of occurrence.

In this world man cannot also achieve free will so that every decision is free of prejudice, vague belief or any irrational influence.

Evolution of probability first started with assigning equal probabilities to events. When *frequentist method* emerged later on, stressed relative frequency of past events to arrive at future outcomes. Finally the subjective approach holds the subjective point of view in terms of personal belief, intuition, superstition and limited knowledge. You will get more bemused when subjectivity intervenes with the randomness of occurrence. In particular when subjective probability encompasses the mass at large, the problem become wider and you may fall into domain of decision by heuristic shortcuts or you will depend entirely on frequency of occurrence of past events, which is never truly representative of future outcome.

Criteria: Rationality may expire on eventualities

We know keeping rationale in all instances being reasonable about outcomes and affected individuals is not that easy, but sometimes evading principles of rationality put us into perplexity. However, if we see over the time horizon, rationality is not static and stubborn thus requires us to draw the practical limit keeping in real-life variables (with respect to time and other factors) in view. Suppose, you are a lawyer and you have given power of attorney by your dying client to form a trust as per his will after his death to donate entire asset to certain organization. And you came suddenly to know after his death that he had hidden facts to his deponents and you about his legal successor for a wrong flimsy reason, you suppress the will to execute for inheritance to his successor's favor. Have you exercised rationality then? It can be explained that your action followed rational path as it is justifiable to underlying reasons.

Consider another example, in case of any road accident, the good Samaritan who helped the deceased or survivor becomes a easy prey to the law of nation and gets harassment. Even the doctor who treats may become suspect for the same reason thus he asks for FIR before treating the patient and the person who brings in gets boiled, even though doctor has exercised his rationale. Now the question is, should the doctor exercise rationale at the cost of life, when his timely action can save him? In such case if the doctor puts an ethical veto into his ruthless rationality, the practical limit is drawn.

Criteria: For every axiom there will be an experiment refuting it.

Since time immemorial science and philosophy have been trying to establish law of the complex universe by emerging axioms and postulates. New horizons get opened up and older principles are getting falsified with respect to newly acquired knowledge. Even if civilization has come long way and heading towards enlightenment, older proven theories comes out be disproved by new evidences. In every point of time which seemed wholesome, exceptions were discovered later on establishing the fact that nothing proves to be eternal in the ravages of time. Constancy of law is challenged by newer facts and experimentation, supporting evidences discovered in the past proved to be insufficient. Why is this happening? Is it because of our lack of completeness of knowledge for which proven and accepted axioms are failing to be time proven? Or are we failing to see subtle fabric of universe constituting every principle for its creation? Answer to these questions will tell us the true story.

Subjective limit in point of no return

Does every subjective limit retain its constancy? The answer is NO. Although, there is a limit to every aspect of our lives, but it is noted to vary from person to person. Suppose, Mr. A has crossed the point of no return according to his belief and Mr. B thinks he could go further. Is there any means to stretch this subjective limit? Let us go into "Addicts' paradigm" which is a purely subjective limit put by the individual.

At any point of time addicts may decide to change himself but likely to continue for some uncertain time. He decides if any sign of bad effect surfaces he would decide to quit. He may or may not see the means of quitting the habit at this stage. He decides to quit and tries hard to find solution how to quit. He prepares himself in quitting his belief that he won't live without this.

He talks about quitting to his companions and try to motivate them in same line. On getting a feasible solution he takes action to quit by reducing or quitting. His initial effort may not be successful if self regulation is not maintained throughout up to the time of reversal.

Reversal may come as original habit; however he may be inspired to change the strategy for further action to start afresh. At this point of time he requires willpower to overcome craving and attracts discomfort of withdrawal effects. Counter good habits or less harmful habits may be created to combat physical craving. Getting rid of environment that promotes indulgence to bad habits may reduce chances of reversal. 'Stop promoter and support inhibitor' approach can help reducing the addiction of bad habit. Therefore, addict's paradigm can only be changed by individual and mostly depends on his/her will power and conscious effort to implement strategy.

Epilogue

Change is eternal

"najayatemriyatevakadacin

nayambhutvabhavitavanabhuyah

ajonityahsasvato 'yam purano

nahanyatehanyamanesharire"-**Bhagavat Gita**

"Everything goes, everything comes back; eternally rolls the wheel of being. Everything dies, everything blossoms again. . . ." -**Friedrich Nietzsche**

Ever since German marine-biology student Christian Sommer, had discovered amazing life cycle of immortal jelly fish while conducting research on hydrozoans, which appeared as defeating the laws of universe about birth, growth, decay and death, it created profound interest to adopt means to achieve human immortality.

In early 90's Sommer went on snorkelling in the deep water of Portofino and gathered hydrozoans from ocean bed. Among the hundreds of organisms he collected a relatively obscure species known to biologists as Turritopsisdohrnii which was later named as immortal jellyfish.

He was perplexed by the life cycles of this species in a manner it refused to die and growing old. Its aging process seemed to appear in reverse direction, growing continually younger until it reaches its initial stage where it begins its life cycle as polyp. Inspired by Sommer's finding, several biologists in Genoa, continued to study the species, and in 1996 they published a paper called "Reversing the Life Cycle."

This finding appeared to have refuted the most fundamental law of the nature that which is born, is bound to die. Isn't it?

Just think of Bhagavat Gita, wherein it described immortality of the soul, that for the soul there is neither birth nor death but it goes on transforming; it is unborn, eternal, ever existing, undying and it does not die with the death of the body. And just think of definition of life and death by medical fraternity, wherein a doctor would certify a person dead when he finds the heart stops beating.

In modern era, it is possible to keep the heart and lung going with the help of artificial life support system. When organ donors die, their organs keep on functioning in other's body. Thus a part of dead person can still live while attaching to another soul.

Think about reproduction of mammals, a foetus is born as a part of living cell of parents and on detaching from its mother's womb, child is born. The child possesses the part of parents' body and thus parents keep alive in their child. So, birth and death of body becomes irrelevant to eternity of soul and therefore cannot be a truth in existence.

The nature's law is not about the life and death of an individual; on the contrary it is for entire kingdom of living and non living matter around it and progress of generation, transformation and towards survival and betterment.

The individual's life depends at his or her willingness to adopt the nature's law, the desire to thrive for continual betterment and flourishing achievement to one's life satisfaction.

Gita also says change is the law of nature. Everything in universe is subjected to change and everything has got to change for its betterment; anything refuses to change will lead` to drop it dead. The refusal of immortal jelly fish to die does not defy the law of eternal changes; it may keep on changing in reverse direction to defy aging, but it would never be static in its lifecycle. You may wonder "why has nature favoured jelly fish with its elusive blessing while it has turned a blind eye to others?"

Being oldest animal with complex organ existent since 700 million years back, we may presume, nature had equipped them with greatest survival kit as they had to sustain their lives till more complex species evolved out of them.

It is the nature's visualization for creation of best creature on earth. And the nature succeeded.

Embrace changes with pleasure, since it's a law of nature that every change has pleasure at the end.

-------------------Let the journey begins----------------------

------------------------Bon Jure------------------------

References and Notes

• Brickman & Campbell (1971). Hedonic relativism and planning the good society. New York: Academic Press. pp. 287–302

• Beja, A. and I. Gilboa (1992), "Numerical Representations of Imperfectly

Ordered Preferences (A Unified Geometric Exposition)", Journal of Mathematical Psychology.

• Einstein Albert: General theory of relativity

• Emma Fletcher, Martha Langley, Free yourself from Anxiety How To Books; Reprint edition (2009) ISBN-10: 1845283112 ISBN-13: 978-1845283117

• Eugine A. Avalon, Theodore Baumeister III Marks' Standard Handbook for Mechanical Engineers, XIth Edition Publisher: McGraw-Hill ISBN:9780071428675

• Fredrickson, BL (2001). "The Role of Positive Emotions in Positive Psychology"

• Goldman, Daniel. Emotional Intelligence and Working with emotional intelligence Penguine books India Pvt. Ltd,(2004) ISBN-13 9780747574569 ISBN-10 0747574561

• Kivosaki, Robert T., Rich Dad Poor Dad, Plata Publishing / Perseus Distribution (2011) ISBN 9781612680019

• Keynes, John Maynard ([1921] 1963), A Treatise on Probability. London: Macmillan.

• Luthans, F.(1973).Organizational behavior. New York: McGraw-Hill. ISBN0-07-125930-9

• Neill Michael, You can have what you want by Hay House; 1 edition (2006) ISBN-10: 1401911838 ISBN-13: 978-1401911836

• Newberry Tommy, Success in not accident , Looking Glass Books (1999) ISBN-10: 1886669090 ISBN-13: 978-1886669093

• Nicholas Shackle: Bertrand's Paradox and the Principle of Indifference

• Schuller, Robert H., Tough times never last, tough people do, Bantam; Reissue edition (1984) ISBN-10: 0553273329 ISBN-13: 978-0553273328

• ShlomoHareli (Dept of psychology-University of Haifa) -Paper presented at ISRE (International society for research on emotions) Toroto, 1996

• Smith E R and Mackie D M, Social psychology (Hove 2007)

• Stephen hawking A brief history of time, bantam press 1989 ISBN 9780553176988

• Stephen hawking The Theory of everything, Jaico Publishing House 2009 ISBN 81-7992-591-9

• Stephen R. Covey, The seven habits of highly effective peopleFree Press; Revised edition (2004) ISBN-10: 0743269519 ISBN-13: 978-0743269513

• Tracy, Brian. Maximum Achievement, Simon & Schuster Publication Year 1993 ISBN-13 9780671865184 ISBN-10 0671865188

• (a): Festinger. L (1957) A theory of cognitive dissonance, Stanford, CA, Stanford University press.andHeider F.(1958) the psychology of interpersonal relations, New York, weily

•(b) Mather, M., Shafir, E., & Johnson, M. K. (2000). Misrememberance of options past: Source monitoring and choice. Psychological Science, 11, 132-138

• (c) Snyder, M. and Cantor, N. (1979), "Testing Hypotheses about Other People: The Use of Historical Knowledge," Journal of Experimental Social Psychology, 15, 330-342

• Fischhoff, B. and Beyth, R. (1975) "I knew it would happen": Remembered probabilities of once-future things. Organizational Behavior and Human Performance, 13, 1-16

• (d) Pronin, E., Lin, D. Y., & Ross, L. (2002). The bias blind spot: Perceptions of bias in self versus others. Personality and Social Psychology Bulletin, 28, 369-381.

• (e) Chung, S. H. and Herrnstein, R. J. (1967). Choice and delay of Reinforcement. Journal of the Experimental Analysis of Behavior, 10 67-64.

• (f) Baron, R. A. and Byrne, D. (1997). Social Psychology, 8th edition. Boston, MA: Allyn and Bacon.

• (g) Savage, L.J. (1954). The Foundations of Statistics. New York, NY: Wiley, Newell, A., & Simon, H. A. (1972). Human problem solving. Englewood Cliffs, NJ: Prentice-Hall

• (h) Kassin, S.M. and Sommers, S.R. (1997). Inadmissible testimony, instructions to disregard, and the jury: substantive versus procedural considerations. Personality and Social Psychology Bulletin, 23, 1046– 54

• Einhorn, H. J. and Hogarth, R. M. (1981). Behavioral decision theory: Processes of judgement and choice. Annual Review of Psychology, 32, 53-88. Hogarth, R. (1987). Judgement and choice (2nd edn.). New York: Wiley.

• (j) Prochaska J.O. (1979). Systems of psychotherapy: a transtheoretical analysis. Homewood, IL: Dorsey Press; Prochaska J.O. and DiClemente C.C. (1982). Trans-theoretical therapy - toward a more integrative model of change. Psychotherapy: Theory, Research and Practice 19(3):276-288.

Web: www.wikipedia.org,

www.google.com,

www.changingmind.org